D1487315

Presented to:

_____

Presented by:

_____

Date:

_____

Prayer serves as an edge and border to
preserve the web of life from unraveling.

Robert Hall

Project developed by Bordon Books, Tulsa, Oklahoma
Concept: Dave Bordon and Tom Winters
Project Writing: Moira Allaby, Elece Hollis, Linda MacKillop, and Rebekah Montgomery in association with SnapdragonGroup℠ Editorial Services

FaithWords
Hachette Book Group USA
1271 Avenue of the Americas, New York, NY 10020

Visit our Web site at www.faithwords.com

Printed in the United States of America

First Edition: November 2006
10 9 8 7 6 5 4 3 2 1

The FaithWords name and loge are trademarks of Hachette Book Group USA.

ISBN=10: 0-446-57937-8
ISBN=13: 978-0-446-57937-7

Anytime
Prayers
FOR
Everyday
Women

New York Boston Nashville

Contents

Prayers of Confession 199

Lifting My Voice to God When I Need Forgiveness

Prayers of Intercession 221
Lifting My Voice to God on Behalf of Others

Prayers for my loved ones:

Prayers for the world around me:

Introduction

God wants to know you—and He wants you to know Him. It's a relationship He has invested His heart in. Does that surprise you? It shouldn't. You are God's most beloved creation, made in His own image. It's natural that He would want to communicate with you, and prayer is the means He has chosen to do just that.

Unfortunately, many women are intimidated by the idea of prayer. God seems so big, so powerful. Why would He care about our puny lives? Why would He want to hear about our troubles or heed our cries for help? The answers to these questions are beyond the scope of our limited understanding, but whatever His reasons, the Bible says He does—care, hear, and answer.

Anytime Prayers for Everyday Women contains the prayers of women just like you—those who have ups and downs of every kind. It is our hope that as you pray along with them within the pages of this book, you will feel God's loving touch on your own life.

I know not by what methods rare,
But this I know: God answers prayer.
I know not if the blessing sought
Will come in just the guise I thought.
I leave my prayer to Him alone
Whose will is wiser than my own.

Eliza M. Hickok

Prayers
of Praise and
Thanksgiving

Lifting My Voice to God
for Who He Is and What He Has
Done for Me

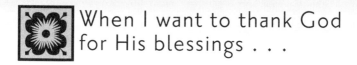

When I want to thank God for His blessings . . .

The faithful will abound with blessings.
PROVERBS 28:20 NRSV

❋

I, the LORD, am the one who answers your prayers and watches over you. . . . Your blessings come from me.
HOSEA 14:8 NCV

❋

[The Lord says] I will make them and the places around My hill a blessing. And I will cause showers to come down in their season; they will be showers of blessing.
EZEKIEL 34:26 NASB

❋

Blessings are on the head of the righteous.
PROVERBS 10:6 RSV

❋

If we are God's children, we will receive blessings from God together with Christ.
ROMANS 8:17 NCV

. . . I will pray.

Dear Lord,

I know there are people far more talented and attractive and wealthy than I, but today I'm aware of how You have blessed my life. Thank You that this morning I woke up in a warm bed in a comfortable and dry home in a safe neighborhood. My cabinets are filled with food, and when I'm sick, an accomplished doctor is available right down the street to care for my needs. In addition to my physical abundance, my life is rich in friends and relationships—people who shower me with concern and care. They defend me in conflicts and carry my hurts as if they were their own wounds. They keep me company, and we laugh together. My job provides for my needs, and all around me pleasures and sights and sounds enrich my life.

Most of all, I'm grateful that You've called me to be a member of Your family. Regardless of what I need, all I have to do is call on You, my heavenly Father, to help me. The greatest blessing of all is knowing that You've rescued me from all my failures by sending Christ as my Savior.

Amen.

There are no days when God's fountain does not flow.

Richard Owen Roberts

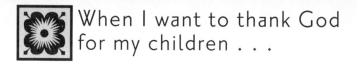# When I want to thank God for my children . . .

May the LORD give you increase,
You and your children.
May you be blessed of the LORD,
Maker of heaven and earth.

PSALM 115:14-15 NASB

Behold, children are a heritage from the LORD,
The fruit of the womb is a reward.
Like arrows in the hand of a warrior,
So are the children of one's youth.
Happy is the man who has his quiver full of them.

PSALM 127:3-5 NKJV

Jesus said, "Let the little children come to me,
and do not hinder them, for the kingdom of heaven
belongs to such as these."

MATTHEW 19:14

Train up a child in the way he should go,
Even when he is old he will not depart from it.

PROVERBS 22:6 NASB

. . . I will pray.

My Heavenly Father,

Amid the chaotic busyness of our everyday lives, You remind me of what a privilege it is to raise my children. Thank You for the rich blessing they are as they noisily run through my house and my days. You know the ways that my heart is tied to theirs, feeling their successes—and their hurts. Thank You for equipping me to raise them.

My children have provided the best years—and the most difficult and exhausting years—of my life; but I'm grateful for the hard work, the companionship, and the fun of raising them. Thank You for the reminder that these years are not permanent so that I appreciate the most mundane moments as well as the frustrating and exhilarating times. Each minute, each hour, and each experience bonds my heart to their hearts. In turn, the pleasures associated with parenting reflect on Your nature and the way that You shower us with gifts.

I'm grateful that You have entrusted me to disciple and care for these young ones. Thank You for the wonderful gift they are to me.

Amen.

One laugh of a child will make the holiest day more sacred still.

Robert Green Ingersoll

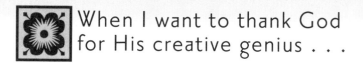

When I want to thank God for His creative genius . . .

God created man in his own image, in the image of God
he created him; male and female he created them.

GENESIS 1:27 NASB

❖

From the time the world was created, people have seen the
earth and sky and all that God made. They can clearly see his
invisible qualities—his eternal power and divine nature.

ROMANS 1:20 NLT

❖

He merely spoke, and the heavens were formed, and all the
galaxies of stars. He made the oceans, pouring them into his
vast reservoirs. Let everyone in all the world—men, women
and children—fear the Lord and stand in awe of him.

PSALM 33:6-8 TLB

❖

What a wildly wonderful world, GOD!
You made it all.

PSALM 104:24 MSG

. . . I will pray.

Dear Mighty God,

I marvel at Your creative genius. My heart swells as I observe the night sky with a sliver of a moon hanging in the midst of colorful clouds. People display creative gifts through the arts, engineering, and intellectual accomplishments, but You are the Author of creativity. Anything created by man simply reflects a tiny portion of Your vast imagination.

The world and this creation show forth Your splendor as the stars move in their heavens and planets rotate in their orbits. The tides and the seas roar and crash, pointing the entire world to You—the invisible but real creative genius working behind the scenes.

Your genius isn't apparent only with the beautiful works of nature and people, though. Often the way You work in our lives and circumstances reflects brilliant and imaginative thinking.

Lord God, help me never to worship the creation but rather worship You as the Creator who gives good gifts for me to enjoy. As the planet bursts forth into colors and all manner of living things, thank You that Your fingerprints can be seen on them all.

Amen.

A true work of art is but a shadow of divine perfection.

Michelangelo

When I want to thank God for His faithfulness . . .

All the paths of the LORD are steadfast love and faithfulness,
for those who keep his covenant and his testimonies.
PSALM 25:10 RSV

❋

I face your Temple as I worship, giving thanks to you for all
your lovingkindness and your faithfulness, for your promises
are backed by all the honor of your name.
PSALM 138:2 TLB

❋

Even when we are too weak to have any faith left,
[Christ] remains faithful to us and will help us,
for he cannot disown us who are part of himself,
and he will always carry out his promises to us.
2 TIMOTHY 2:13 TLB

❋

Your love, O LORD, reaches to the heavens,
your faithfulness to the skies.
PSALM 36:5

❋

I will proclaim the name of the LORD;
how glorious is our God!
DEUTERONOMY 32:3 NLT

. . . I will pray.

Dear Steadfast Lord,

As much as I love my friends and family, there are times when I haven't come through for them. My own failure and lack of faithfulness, however, shine a light on Your steady and true nature—how You never let Your people down. I'm a bundle of good intentions, but You are more than a God of good intentions. You are the faithful Father who keeps Your commitments to us.

Many times, I have put all my trust in You, Your character, and Your Word, hoping and waiting for a situation to turn out right. And after years of walking with You, I have learned that You always come through for Your children; You've never been untrue to Your Word. In some cases, You haven't been speedy or worked out the situation according to my plan, but You've always been a Promise Keeper. I praise You, Father, for all the ways in which You have been faithful and true—not just to me, but to all of Your children throughout all time.

As I continue to grow in my walk with You, help me to become more faithful so that I can fully reflect Your nature to others.

Amen.

In God's faithfulness lies eternal security.

Corrie ten Boom

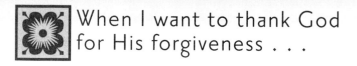

When I want to thank God for His forgiveness . . .

If You, LORD, should mark iniquities,
O Lord, who could stand?
But there is forgiveness with You.
PSALM 130:3-4 NASB

❀

Come now, and let us reason together, saith the LORD: though
your sins be as scarlet, they shall be as white as snow; though
they be red like crimson, they shall be as wool.
ISAIAH 1:18 KJV

❀

Bless the LORD, O my soul,
And forget not all His benefits:
Who forgives all your iniquities, . . .
Who redeems your life from destruction,
Who crowns you with lovingkindness and tender mercies.
PSALM 103:2-4 NKJV

❀

If we confess our sins, he is faithful and just, and will forgive
our sins and cleanse us from all unrighteousness.
1 JOHN 1:9 RSV

. . . I will pray.

Dear Savior,

I blew it today, and there's no one to blame but myself. My actions drew me into a mess that I should've known to avoid. If only I had not given in to the temptation to indulge in pride and selfishness. At times like this, I want to hide my face from You and run from Your presence. But just when I'm sure You want to run from me, too, I feel the gentle tug of Your presence. You remind me that You are the God who forgives broken people like me who come humbly to You.

Lord, I come.

Thank You for a second chance and a fresh start. In the world without You, bad decisions result in waste and brokenness with no hope for repair. In the spiritual world, though, brokenness is often the beginning of an entirely new and restored relationship between You and Your people—once we've turned away from wrong behavior. Only a truly merciful and loving God would accept fallen people like us.

Thank You for Your forgiving Spirit who draws me back and gives me a second chance.

Amen.

When God pardons, He consigns the offense
to everlasting forgetfulness.

Merv Rosell

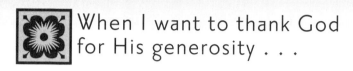# When I want to thank God for His generosity . . .

To him who is able to do immeasurably more than all we ask or imagine, according to his power that is at work within us, to him be glory in the church.

EPHESIANS 3:20-21

❀

Generous to a fault, you [God] lavish your favor on all creatures.

PSALM 145:16 MSG

❀

All sunshine and sovereign is GOD, generous in gifts and glory. He doesn't scrimp with his traveling companions.

PSALM 84:11 MSG

❀

Splendor and beauty mark his craft; His generosity never gives out. His miracles are his memorial.

PSALM 111:3-4 MSG

. . . I will pray.

Dear Lord,

Sometimes when people ask favors of me, I feel that my response to them is stingy. Sometimes I even feel resentful that they require the amount that they do. I know this attitude reflects a sense of poverty in my heart.

In sharp contrast to my miserly ways is the great generosity that You've shown to me. My hands are so full because of how You lavishly pour out answers. When I whispered a prayer a while back, I included my vision of how the prayer should be answered. But You came running to me in a way that did so much more! Meeting the need in the way that You wanted, You poured out a response that reflected Your great love and Your delight in giving us good gifts. There's certainly no stinginess on Your part.

Thank You for Your great spirit of generosity and for how You give above and beyond what we need or ask. Help me to develop that giving spirit so that I might reflect just a little of it—no, a lot of it—to other people. I praise You for Your abundant goodness to me.

Amen.

Accustom yourself to the wonderful thought that God loves you with a tenderness, a generosity, and an intimacy that surpasses all your dreams.

Abbe Henri de Tourville

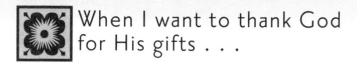

When I want to thank God for His gifts . . .

Every good and perfect gift is from above,
coming down from the Father of the heavenly lights,
who does not change like shifting shadows.
JAMES 1:17

Concerning spiritual gifts, . . . sisters, I do not want you to be
uninformed. . . . There are varieties of gifts, but the same
Spirit; and there are varieties of services, but the same Lord;
and there are varieties of activities, but it is the same God
who activates all of them in everyone. To each is given the
manifestation of the Spirit for the common good.
1 CORINTHIANS 12:1, 4-7 NRSV

Just as we have many members in one body and all the
members do not have the same function, so we, who are
many, are one body in Christ, and individually members one
of another. Since we have gifts that differ according to the
grace given to us, each of us is to exercise them accordingly.
ROMANS 12:4-6 NASB

. . . I will pray.

Dear Heavenly Father,

Many people come across my path every day—at work, at church, through phone calls, and by e-mail. Whenever I am having a tough time, I'm so aware of how You send just the right people to represent Yourself by sharing their God-given gifts with me and by putting hands and feet to Your teachings.

When I've needed it, people have come to me and instructed me in situations where I needed the wisdom of a discerning teacher and counselor. You've sent friends who have sat by my side during particularly long and depressing waiting periods, when I needed a comforting and merciful presence. You've sent others to speak to me and exhort me to look at my self-defeating behaviors.

I'm so grateful that You are the Creator and the Sender of good gifts and that Your generosity is one of the ways in which You provide for us and come to our rescue. I praise You for making Your presence known to me by sending people with gifts to minister to my needs and brokenness.

Amen.

God is so good that He only awaits our desire
to overwhelm us with the gift of Himself.

François Fénelon

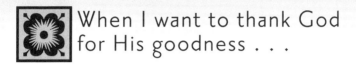

When I want to thank God for His goodness . . .

The LORD is good to all,
And His mercies are over all His works.

PSALM 145:9 NASB

※

I am still confident of this:
I will see the goodness of the LORD
in the land of the living.

PSALM 27:13

※

How great is your goodness,
which you have stored up for those who fear you,
which you bestow in the sight of men
on those who take refuge in you.

PSALM 31:19

※

In his goodness he chose to make us his own children by
giving us his true word. And we, out of all creation, became
his choice possession.

JAMES 1:18 NLT

. . . I will pray.

Dear Sovereign Lord,

In strong contrast to the way humans let each other down, Your goodness is all around me, expressed in Your righteous heart attitude toward me. Many children grow up thinking adults are unreliable and untrustworthy because of earthly parents who fail to communicate love and who lack goodness. You are so different, though. You never fail, and the goodness in Your character never changes. Your eyes are always turned on me—watching me, thinking of me, remembering me, helping me grow, and sending me good things.

Thank You for putting my needs so high on Your priority list. Because Your character is just and never harsh or impatient, I learn to lean heavily on You with the weight of a weary child.

One of my greatest needs is the reassurance that You love me no matter what I've done wrong in the past or how I'll act in the future. You are truly a good God who even runs to people who are running full speed away from You! Thank You for seeking me out and sending me so many chances to notice Your love and hear Your voice.

Amen.

The Lord's goodness surrounds us at every moment.
I walk through it almost with difficulty, as through
thick grass and flowers.

R. W. Barbour

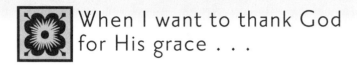

When I want to thank God for His grace . . .

The amazing grace of the Master, Jesus Christ,
the extravagant love of God, the intimate friendship of
the Holy Spirit, be with all of you.

2 CORINTHIANS 13:14 MSG

From his fullness we have all received, grace upon grace.
The law indeed was given through Moses; grace and
truth came through Jesus Christ.

JOHN 1:16-17 NRSV

Even though on the outside it often looks like things are falling
apart on us, on the inside, where God is making new life,
not a day goes by without his unfolding grace.

2 CORINTHIANS 4:16 MSG

Now God has us where he wants us, with all the time in this
world and the next to shower grace and kindness upon us in
Christ Jesus.

EPHESIANS 2:7 MSG

. . . I will pray.

Dear Merciful God,

When I am wronged by others, help me to bring You the offenses and lay them at Your feet. Help me to forgive and let go so that I can leave the incident in the past and continue forward with the person as if the hurt had never taken place. Help me to extend that unmerited favor that You so graciously offer to me.

When I've fallen into wrong behavior, You've scooped me out of it to start fresh with a clean slate. Despite my feelings of guilt, You behave toward me as if You have no memory of the wrongs I've done. Even better than simply forgetting my past, you usher me into Your presence and treat me like a beloved child, restoring everything that I've broken.

Thank You, Father, for that truly amazing grace—so large and bountiful, able to cover all my fallen ways. I know that I don't deserve to have my punishment excused, but that's how You treat me—giving me a life filled with peace and a restored relationship.

Amen.

Grace is given not because we have done good works,
but in order that we may be able to do them.

Saint Augustine of Hippo

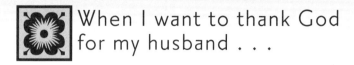

When I want to thank God for my husband . . .

Let the wife see that she respects and reverences her husband [that she notices him, regards him, honors him, prefers him, venerates, and esteems him; and that she defers to him, praises him, and loves and admires him exceedingly].

EPHESIANS 5:33 AMP

She comforts, encourages, and does [her husband] only good as long as there is life within her.

PROVERBS 31:12 AMP

Her husband is known in the [city's] gates, when he sits among the elders of the land.

PROVERBS 31:23 AMP

Together with your reverence [for your husband; you are to feel for him all that reverence includes: to respect, defer to, revere him—to honor, esteem, appreciate, prize, and, in the human sense, to adore him, that is, to admire, praise, be devoted to, deeply love, and enjoy your husband].

1 PETER 3:2 AMP

. . . I will pray.

Dear Lord,

When I think about my husband, my heart is filled with so much love for him. He possesses so many qualities that I admire. In short, You have given me the man who is perfect for me. His temperament complements mine so well that it's obvious there's been a divine match at work here.

You've provided him as my traveling companion with whom I can share the trials and joys of life, raising children, and growing in You. The road hasn't all been smooth, and there have been times when we wondered if we would make it. Some days we still struggle with each other and take each other for granted. Most days, though, he's my best friend, and I know that our relationship is a testimony of Your work in this broken world.

Thank You for his hard work and what he provides for our family. Over the years You have so knit our hearts together that often only a glance across a crowded room reveals a shared secret, a private joke, a hidden thought. You've been there all these years helping two become one. Thank You for the gift of my husband.

Amen.

Chains do not hold a marriage together. It is threads, hundreds of tiny threads that sew people together through the years.
Simone Signoret

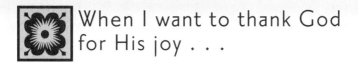

When I want to thank God for His joy . . .

[Nehemiah said] The joy of the LORD is your strength.
NEHEMIAH 8:10 NASB

❋

[The Lord says] The joy of the LORD will fill you to
overflowing. You will glory in the Holy One of Israel.
ISAIAH 41:16 NLT

❋

Be full of joy in the Lord always.
I will say again, be full of joy.
PHILIPPIANS 4:4 NCV

❋

You shall go out with joy,
And be led out with peace;
The mountains and the hills
Shall break forth into singing before you,
And all the trees of the field shall clap their hands.
ISAIAH 55:12 NKJV

A joyful heart is good medicine,
But a broken spirit dries up the bones.
PROVERBS 17:22 NASB

. . . I will pray.

Dear Heavenly Father,

In the past, I haven't always been known as a person who is giddy and happy. To be perfectly blunt, sometimes I'm moody and very serious. Over these recent years, though, friends and family have noticed a difference in me that they name as joy. I know where it comes from: my new joy comes from knowing You.

In the past, I'd show joy when things were going my way and sailing along smoothly. When I got a raise at work, I felt "joy." When there was a new man in my life, I felt "joy." When I lost that extra fifteen pounds after the holiday, I felt "joy." Now my new attitude is different from that old "joy," because right now there are many challenges facing me. Right in the midst of these challenges, though, I've been experiencing joy. I know this can't be an attitude that I've created myself. That means You are responsible for the presence of joy in my life, and You are the Creator and Giver of joy.

Thank You for sending this different spirit, and for all the work You're doing in my life that produces joy.

Amen.

I have no understanding of a long-faced Christian. If God is anything, He must be joy.

Joe E. Brown

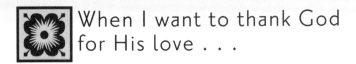 # When I want to thank God for His love . . .

If anyone obeys his word, God's love is truly made complete in him. This is how we know we are in him.

1 JOHN 2:5

May the Lord lead your hearts into God's love.

2 THESSALONIANS 3:5 NCV

This is what real love is: It is not our love for God; it is God's love for us in sending his Son to be the way to take away our sins.

1 JOHN 4:10 NCV

God's love has been poured into our hearts through the Holy Spirit which has been given to us.

ROMANS 5:5 RSV

God's love will continue forever.

PSALM 52:1 NCV

. . . I will pray.

Dear Loving Lord,

In this country, You've demonstrated love to us by showering us with Your favor for centuries. We are covered with the blessings of fruitful living, freedom from tyranny, bountiful harvests, and a prosperous economy. Our government provides security and protection for us. We are surrounded with beauty from coast to coast; inland, we enjoy mountains and canyons and green valleys that please the eye and the soul because You choose to love us through gifts.

In my own life, I've received the same kind of favor poured out to me—and even more. That love and favor comes in the form of Your counsel to me, Your protection of me, Your patience with me, Your salvation and gifts to me. When I'm going astray, You stop me in my tracks and draw me back into the fold. I see all these blessings as coming from You who directs my path and cares for me throughout my life.

Thank You for seeing me in all my forms—weak and strong, lovely and unlovely, obedient and disobedient—and loving me anyway. Humbly I adore You, Lord, for Your loving nature.

Amen.

God does not love us because we are valuable.
We are valuable because God loves us.

Archbishop Fulton J. Sheen

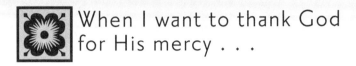 When I want to thank God
for His mercy . . .

All those who know your mercy, Lord, will count on you for
help. For you have never yet forsaken those who trust in you.
PSALM 9:10 TLB

I will always trust in you and in your mercy and
shall rejoice in your salvation. I will sing to the Lord
because he has blessed me so richly.
PSALM 13:5-6 TLB

The steadfast love of the LORD never ceases,
his mercies never come to an end;
they are new every morning;
great is thy faithfulness.
LAMENTATIONS 3:22-23 RSV

God is sheer mercy and grace;
not easily angered, he's rich in love.
PSALM 103:8 MSG

. . . I will pray.

Dear Lord God,

The world around me is filled with people suffering. They are people in prison, children in need of school clothes, parents worrying about what tomorrow will bring for their families, and those thirsty for counsel and direction. In the midst of all these situations, I know You have a merciful heart that is turned toward the poor in spirit and the hurting. I thank You for that mercy and for the way You use Your people to express compassion to others.

Many times I've been shown Your mercy, whether I needed a job or I had a physical need and felt all alone. Thank You for Your compassionate kindness that sends people to comfort as well as Your comforting Holy Spirit. You carry all my hurts and save my tears. You are constantly beholding my face.

Thank You for all of Your tender mercies toward me, Father. Give me eyes to see others in need and a heart that overflows with Your mercy to them. Praise Your name.

Amen.

Mercy . . . is a good thing, for it makes men perfect, in that it imitates the perfect Father. Nothing graces the Christian soul as much as mercy.

Saint Ambrose

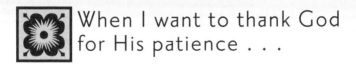

When I want to thank God for His patience . . .

The fruit of the Spirit is . . . patience.
GALATIANS 5:22 NASB

❋

With patience you can convince a ruler,
and a gentle word can get through to the hard-headed.
PROVERBS 25:15 NCV

❋

The Lord is not slow about His promise, as some count
slowness, but is patient toward you, not wishing for any to
perish but for all to come to repentance.
2 PETER 3:9 NASB

❋

God had mercy on me, so that Christ Jesus could use me as a
prime example of his great patience with even the worst
sinners.
1 TIMOTHY 1:16 NLT

❋

The patient in spirit is better than the proud in spirit.
ECCLESIASTES 7:8 RSV

. . . I will pray.

Dear Savior,

I am so disappointed in myself when I show an impatient heart or tongue. I don't mean to do it, but with the demands of life and work and responsibilities, sometimes I feel everything crowding in on me. Those are just excuses, though, aren't they?

My short-fused temperament is so different from Your long-fused and patient one. I'm so grateful that You patiently wait for me to return when I've strayed or when I need to apologize to someone whom I have wronged. Patiently You watch me while I live a life walking too close to the line of trouble. As a gentle Teacher, You patiently proceed to tell this student the same instructions over and over again, never complaining about having to repeat the lesson one more time.

I'm thankful that Your Spirit is the opposite of my impatient one. I'd like my fuse to grow and duplicate Yours so that I avoid hypocritically tapping into Your bountiful patience while I withhold it from others. Even though I don't deserve Your patient care and concern, You show it to me anyway, and I am thankful.

Amen.

Our ground of hope is that God
does not weary of mankind.

Ralph Washington Sockman

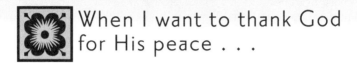

When I want to thank God for His peace . . .

Following after the Holy Spirit leads to life and peace.
ROMANS 8:6 TLB

*Don't worry about anything; instead, pray about everything;
tell God your needs and don't forget to thank him for his
answers. If you do this you will experience God's peace, which
is far more wonderful than the human mind can understand.
His peace will keep your thoughts and your hearts
quiet and at rest as you trust in Christ Jesus.*
PHILIPPIANS 4:6-7 TLB

*[Jesus said] I am leaving you with a gift—peace of mind and
heart! And the peace I give isn't fragile like the peace the
world gives. So don't be troubled or afraid.*
JOHN 14:27 TLB

*Let the peace of heart which comes from Christ be
always present in your hearts and lives, for this is your
responsibility and privilege as members of his body.
And always be thankful.*
COLOSSIANS 3:15 TLB

. . . I will pray.

Dear God,

Anything that could go wrong has gone wrong lately. Major disruptions have entered my life and caught me off guard. At night I lie awake, mulling over the recent events, tossing and turning in bed when I should be sleeping. I desperately need Your peace.

What good is Your peace, after all, if I experience it only when the going is good and the road is smooth? This is really the time when true peace is needed—when I should lean on You and put all my trust in You. In the rush of trying to fix one problem after another, I've not focused on You enough.

Something amazing happens when I finally put my cares on Your shoulders—real peace shows up, unexpected and deep in my soul, allowing me to experience a calm that is otherworldly. Even if nothing changes in challenging circumstances, Your peace stabilizes my emotions and keeps me focused on You. This ability to respond to hardships with quiet confidence is something bigger than myself and can come only from You. I receive Your peace now and thank You for it.

Amen.

Finding God, you have no need to seek peace,
for He himself is your peace.

Frances J. Roberts

When I want to thank God for His presence . . .

Wonderful times of refreshment will come from the presence of the Lord.

ACTS 3:20 NLT

❋

God has made you his friends again. He did this through Christ's death in the body so that he might bring you into God's presence as people who are holy.

COLOSSIANS 1:22 NCV

❋

Be still in the presence of the LORD, and wait patiently for him to act.

PSALM 37:7 NLT

❋

Let us come before His presence with thanksgiving.

PSALM 95:2 NKJV

❋

And He said, "My presence shall go with you, and I will give you rest."

EXODUS 33:14 NASB

. . . I will pray.

Dear Father,

Thank You for the gift of knowing that You are with me always. From my younger years until today, You have been by my side, Your ear always open to my call. This is one of those times, Father, when I really need to sense Your presence.

Even though my heart is lonely, it comforts me to know You are here. Your presence blows in at these times and reminds my heart that You are as real and palpable as the fall breeze coming through my window. When I quiet myself and whisper a prayer to You, I'm reminded that You are very close—as close as the mention of Your name.

Thank You for the gift of Your presence in the form of the Holy Spirit who keeps me company while drawing me into Your presence through worship. At these precious times, I am so aware of You, and I hear Your voice speaking words of encouragement to my heart. The rest of the world slips into the background of my mind, and You are the focus in the forefront. Thank You for allowing me to bask in Your presence.

Amen.

As His child, you are entitled to His kingdom,
the warmth, the peace, and the power of
His presence.

Author Unknown

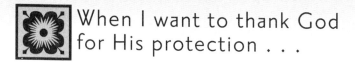

When I want to thank God for His protection . . .

Let all who take refuge in you be glad;
let them ever sing for joy.
Spread your protection over them,
that those who love your name may rejoice in you.
PSALM 5:11

The LORD loves the just
and will not forsake his faithful ones.
They will be protected forever.
PSALM 37:28

Happy are those who trust him for protection.
PSALM 2:12 NCV

He shall give His angels charge over you,
To keep you in all your ways.
PSALM 91:11 NKJV

. . . I will pray.

Dear God,

Thank You for Your protection! How many times You have watched over me and kept me from danger. I'm sure I won't know about some of them until I get to heaven. Then there are the times I do know about—like the times I've accidentally done something stupid while driving my car. Thank You for watching over me and helping me avoid a huge catastrophe.

This can be a frightening world, and we are surrounded by danger on all sides, but I rest in the midst of Your covering that is draped over me. Thank You for surrounding me with angels for my protection. Knowing that nothing will come into my life that You can't handle is a comforting thought.

When I send my loved ones out into the world, I can't always be there with them to run in front of every danger and rescue them from harm, but I can leave them in Your strong and capable hands. Thank You, Father, for the way You watch over us and protect us.

Amen.

Angels are God's secret service agents.
Their assignment—our protection.

Meriwether Williams

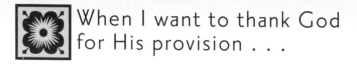 When I want to thank God
for His provision . . .

I have been young, and now am old,
yet I have not seen the righteous forsaken
or their children begging bread.
PSALM 37:25 NRSV

My God shall supply all your need according to
his riches in glory by Christ Jesus.
PHILIPPIANS 4:19 KJV

[Jesus said] Don't worry about food—what to eat and drink;
don't worry at all that God will provide it for you. All
mankind scratches for its daily bread, but your heavenly
Father knows your needs. He will always give you all you
need from day to day if you will make the Kingdom of God
your primary concern.
LUKE 12:29-31 TLB

He provides food for those who fear him;
he is ever mindful of his covenant.
PSALM 111:5 RSV

. . . I will pray.

Dear God and Provider,

I've been struggling with my finances lately, as You know, Lord. The price of everything from gas to a loaf of bread is rising, and then there are medical expenses, automobile and home repairs, insurance, and a myriad of other things crying out for my salary, which doesn't seem to cover it all.

Instead of focusing on all these pressing needs, I want to focus on the things that You've so richly provided for me. I woke up this morning to warm coffee brewing in the kitchen. A steaming shower greeted me in my home where the furnace chugged out comfortable air to shelter me from the cold weather outside. Friends call to check on me, sending me the warmth of their care. And Your presence is ever with me, meeting the deepest longings of my heart.

Forgive me for letting financial pressure get to me. You've always provided the things I need—not to mention the desires of my heart that You've granted. I know that because I'm Your child, I'll never lack the things I need. Thank you for your faithful provision.

Amen.

God is absolutely unlimited in His ability and His resources. And He is unlimited in His desire to pour out those resources upon us.

Gloria Copeland

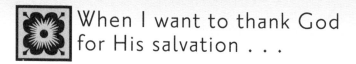

When I want to thank God for His salvation . . .

*I am not ashamed of the gospel: it is the power of God
for salvation to every one who has faith.*

ROMANS 1:16 RSV

❀

*I tell you, now is the time of God's favor,
now is the day of salvation.*

2 CORINTHIANS 6:2

❀

*The LORD lives, and blessed be my rock;
And exalted be the God of my salvation.*

PSALM 18:46 NASB

❀

*[Peter said] Jesus is the only One who can save people. His
name is the only power in the world that has been given to
save people. We must be saved through him.*

ACTS 4:12 NCV

❀

*If you confess with your mouth the Lord Jesus and believe in
your heart that God has raised Him from the dead, you will
be saved.*

ROMANS 10:9 NKJV

. . . I will pray.

My Dear Savior,

Thank You, Lord, for my memory, which allows me to realize what life would've been like if You hadn't come into my darkened and broken world to rescue me. Before You saved me, my choices were harmful and my path was headed for destruction. My days and nights were meaningless and hopeless. Risky behavior and negative, unhealthy relationships inundated my life.

Then one day You burst onto the scene and showed me that I needed to be saved from my nature and myself. When I look back, I realize You loved me enough to come and find me and give me a new heart. Now Your Holy Spirit rules me, and I feel as if Your favor covers and protects me like a shawl. Each day, I become more like You in character.

I know I didn't deserve the gift of salvation, and I'm filled with gratitude. Since the day of my new birth, You've been working to reshape my vision of family, work, and service to now include Your plan. My heart sings with praise to a God who comes to find His lost children and brings them home at such great cost to Himself.

Amen.

It is not your hold of Christ that saves you,
but His hold of you!

Charles Haddon Spurgeon

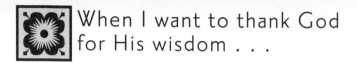

When I want to thank God for His wisdom . . .

Just as the heavens are higher than the earth,
so are my ways higher than your ways
and my thoughts higher than your thoughts.
ISAIAH 55:9 NCV

God's wisdom is deep, and his power is great.
JOB 9:4 NCV

Fools think their own way is right,
but the wise listen to advice.
PROVERBS 12:15 NRSV

Wisdom will make your life pleasant
and will bring you peace.
As a tree produces fruit,
wisdom gives life to those who use it,
and everyone who uses it will be happy.
PROVERBS 3:17-18 NCV

. . . I will pray.

Dear Wise Father,

   If it had been my choice, I would have made the situation work out differently. My planning and imagination held a more favorable outcome—to me. My heart wouldn't have been disappointed, and time never would have been wasted. Then I remember Your wisdom and how it is so high above my own thinking and vantage point.

   While I'm blinded to the larger picture, You are all-wise and knowing. I don't understand how circumstances and events fit together like the pieces to a perfect puzzle, but You understand. I don't want to experience pain, yet in Your wisdom, You turn every disappointment and circumstance into something good. Thank You for Your ways and Your wisdom that rise above my thinking—despite my thinking. Sometimes I come kicking and screaming to wisdom, willing to settle for mediocrity so that I won't have to endure discomfort.

   Thank You for preventing me from simply settling for anything other than Your best. When I sit before You, reading Your Word, waiting for Your answers, and taking my hands off of situations, wisdom shows up.

   Amen.

Most of us go through life praying a little, planning a little, . . . always secretly afraid that we will miss the way. . . . There is a better way. It is to repudiate our own wisdom and take instead the infinite wisdom of God.

A. W. Tozer

Were half the breath that's vainly spent,
To heaven in supplication sent,
Our cheerful song would oftener be,
"Hear what the Lord has done for me."

Garnet Rolling

Prayers of Supplication

Lifting My Voice to God
When I Need Help

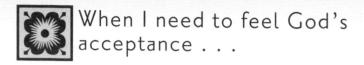

When I need to feel God's acceptance . . .

The God and Father of our Lord Jesus Christ
. . . made us accepted in the Beloved.
EPHESIANS 1:3, 6 NKJV

❀

[Jesus said] The one who comes to Me
I will certainly not cast out.
JOHN 6:37 NASB

❀

Christ accepted you, so you should accept each other,
which will bring glory to God.
ROMANS 15:7 NCV

❀

If you want favor with both God and man, and a reputation
for good judgment and common sense, then trust the Lord
completely.
PROVERBS 3:4-5 TLB

❀

You bless the righteous, O LORD;
you cover them with favor as with a shield.
PSALM 5:12 NRSV

. . . I will pray.

Dear Lord,

Often I feel that I don't fit in anywhere—not at work, not in my church, not in my family, not with my friends. Does anyone understand me and accept me the way I am today? Does anyone understand how my background and experiences have influenced me and made me into this present-day self? Sometimes the rejection—both real and imagined—makes me feel unlovable, not just unloved.

During the times when it's difficult to find a friend or a family member who accepts me with all my foibles and rough edges, I need to turn my mind to You. You know me in the depth of my being and see where I came from, as well as who I will become in the future. In You, I'm accepted and I fit in without having to be a finished product today.

My heart is filled with gratitude for that rare love. Thank You that no matter how I feel, Your love remains the same and is not dependent on either my actions or my emotions. You know me as I really am—the person You created.

Amen.

God, our wise and creative Maker, has been pleased to make everyone different and no one perfect. The sooner we appreciate and accept that fact, the deeper we will appreciate and accept one another, just as our Designer planned us.

Charles R. Swindoll

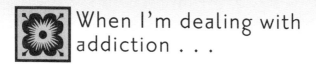 # When I'm dealing with addiction . . .

Behold, the eye of the LORD is on those who fear Him,
On those who hope in His mercy,
To deliver their soul from death,
And to keep them alive in famine.
PSALM 33:18-19 NKJV

[The Lord] sent from on high, He took me;
He drew me out of many waters.
He delivered me from my strong enemy,
And from those who hated me, for they were too mighty for
me.
PSALM 18:16-17 NASB

On God rests my deliverance and my honor;
my mighty rock, my refuge is God.
PSALM 62:7 RSV

Sin will have no dominion over you,
since you are . . . under grace.
ROMANS 6:14 RSV

. . . I will pray.

Dear God,

How did I ever get to this place? My struggle begins from the moment I wake up as I wrestle with the pull of my addiction. From early morning until late at night, my mind is bombarded with temptation. I'm told to take it one day at a time, but sometimes I have to take it one minute at a time.

Lord, I need You to save me from the life created by this addiction. I need Your power to break the hold that the taunting thoughts have on my mind. I'm feeling very weak, but I hear that when I am at my weakest point, You are strong. Today help me keep my mind on Your help that is more than adequate rather than on how I can numb my pain. Give me grace to turn my eyes to You, my God and Savior, for all my emotional and spiritual needs. Fill me with courage to accept no substitute, and give me strength to seek professional help when I need it.

There is no need to focus on any replacement for You, God. All that I will ever need is in You. Help me to walk that out in practical ways today and every day.

Amen.

Father, set me free in the glory of Thy will,
so that I will only as Thou willest. . . . Thou alone art
deliverance—absolute safety from every cause and
kind of trouble that ever existed, anywhere now exists,
or ever can exist in Thy universe.

George MacDonald

When I'm feeling anger . . .

Patience is better than strength.
Controlling your temper is better than capturing a city.
PROVERBS 16:32 NCV

Put them all aside: anger, wrath, malice, slander,
and abusive speech from your mouth.
COLOSSIANS 3:8 NASB

Refrain from anger and turn from wrath;
do not fret—it leads only to evil.
PSALM 37:8

Do not be quickly provoked in your spirit,
for anger resides in the lap of fools.
ECCLESIASTES 7:9

You must understand this, my beloved: let everyone be quick
to listen, slow to speak, slow to anger; for your anger does not
produce God's righteousness.
JAMES 1:19-20 NRSV

. . . I will pray.

Dear Father God,

I find it difficult to concentrate today because angry feelings are flooding my thoughts and my heart. The challenging part is that more than one incident has angered me. My emotions seem to be out of control so that anyone or anything that comes into my path today meets with my fury.

You are the only one capable of helping me get to the root cause of this anger, and I ask You to do so. You are the only one who truly heals and restores, and I ask You to do that as well.

Help me keep in mind that I have the potential to commit acts that anger others too. In those times, I'm desperate for forgiveness and understanding. Please calm my emotions and bathe me in Your peace.

Thank You for Your Word, which has the power to replace negative thoughts and damaging emotions with positive thoughts and healthy emotions that are more pleasing to You— and beneficial to me. Thank You for the peace and self-control that are mine through the fruit of the Spirit.

Amen.

When angry, take a lesson from technology;
always count down before blasting off.

Author Unknown

When I need answers . . .

Your word is a lamp to my feet
And a light to my path.
<small>PSALM 119:105 NKJV</small>

Lord, hear my prayer! Listen to my plea!
Don't turn away from me in this time of my distress.
Bend down your ear and give me speedy answers.
<small>PSALM 102:1-2 TLB</small>

Listen to this prayer of mine, GOD;
pay attention to what I'm asking.
Answer me—you're famous for your answers!
Do what's right for me.
<small>PSALM 143:1 MSG</small>

I cry aloud to the LORD,
and he answers me from his holy hill.
<small>PSALM 3:4 RSV</small>

. . . I will pray.

Dear Wise Father,

Today I find myself in several situations where I am in desperate need of answers. These circumstances make no sense. I have gone to wise counselors, mature Christian friends, and devoted loved ones, but no one seems to have the help that I desperately need. I have read books and researched the experts and still I come up clueless. Now I turn to You.

This is new ground to me; I've never been here before. I need You to shine a light on this path to show me the way to go, providing wisdom so that I know what my next step should be—or if there should be a next step. I read Your Word so that You can instruct me. Send the answers to me, or send me to the answers.

Thank You for the great comfort in my heart from knowing You hold all the solutions to the questions and problems that stump me in life. I come to You in humble dependence and look to You, knowing and trusting that You will provide all the answers I need.

Amen.

God has never turned away the questions
of a sincere searcher.

Max L. Lucado

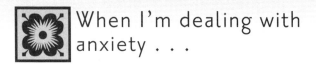

When I'm dealing with anxiety . . .

When anxiety was great within me,
your consolation brought joy to my soul.

PSALM 94:19

❀

Cast all your anxiety on him because he cares for you.

1 PETER 5:7

❀

Anxiety weighs down the human heart,
but a good word cheers it up.

PROVERBS 12:25 NRSV

❀

Be anxious for nothing, but in everything by prayer and
supplication, with thanksgiving, let your requests be made
known to God; and the peace of God, which surpasses all
understanding, will guard your hearts and minds through
Christ Jesus.

PHILIPPIANS 4:6-7 NKJV

❀

May God bless you richly and grant you increasing freedom
from all anxiety and fear.

1 PETER 1:2 TLB

. . . I will pray.

Dear Lord,

Sometimes I let anxiety ruin my day. I fret about keeping my loved ones and myself safe. I'm ashamed to say I fret about the future even though You tell us not to worry about tomorrow. You don't want me to waste my days worrying over disasters that might never arise.

Instead of behaving like a frightened child, concentrating on the bad, I choose to focus my thinking on Your ability to manage my circumstances. All of my anxieties calm in Your presence when I sit at Your feet, leaving each care there, trusting that You'll equip me and bring me through each experience I encounter. As I remember Your great power and ability to rule the universe, I realize how silly my anxiety appears.

Many situations might never become as bad as I imagine, and for the hard times that do arise, Your grace will be more than adequate. Help me to live in the present rather than the future of "what if." I give to You all of my concerns, and in their place, I receive Your peace.

Amen.

Man's world has become a nervous one,
encompassed by anxiety. God's world is other than
this; always balanced, calm, and in order.

Faith Baldwin

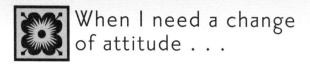

When I need a change of attitude . . .

A relaxed attitude lengthens life.
PROVERBS 14:30 NLT

❋

*The Kingdom of God is not a matter of what we
eat or drink, but of living a life of goodness and peace and
joy in the Holy Spirit. If you serve Christ with this attitude,
you will please God.*
ROMANS 14:17-18 NLT

❋

*May God, who gives this patience and encouragement, help
you live in complete harmony with each other—each with the
attitude of Christ Jesus toward the other.*
ROMANS 15:5 NLT

❋

*Be made new in the attitude of your minds; and . . .
put on the new self, created to be like God in true
righteousness and holiness.*
EPHESIANS 4:23

❋

*The word of God is living and active. . . . It judges the
thoughts and attitudes of the heart.*
HEBREWS 4:12

. . . I will pray.

Merciful Father,

I'm in need of an attitude adjustment. I've been wallowing in emotions that will only harm me and prevent me from being an effective witness for You. Also, I have taken my frustrations out on my family with my negative mind-set and words.

Forgive me, Lord, and soften my bad attitude—toward You, toward others, toward my circumstances. Thank You for reminding me that I'm not an orphan who doesn't have a Father in heaven who loves her. You love me more than I'm capable of loving anyone else, so please replace this godless viewpoint with one that is pleasing to You. I might not be able to change the circumstances, but I can change how I view them and how I respond to them. It's my strongest desire to take advantage of this opportunity to know You better and to see You work. Give me Your perspective and help me to change deep inside so that I have a Christlike attitude.

Thank You for the attitude that Jesus modeled. He always loved, always trusted, always hoped, always obeyed. Make me more like Jesus, I pray.

Amen.

God . . . gives me the freedom to acknowledge my negative attitudes . . . but not the freedom to act them out because they are as destructive for me as they are for the other person.

Rebecca Manley Pippert

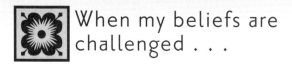 # When my beliefs are challenged . . .

Your godly lives will speak to them better than any words.
They will be won over by watching your pure, godly behavior.
1 PETER 3:1-2 NLT

I pray for you constantly, asking God, the glorious Father
of our Lord Jesus Christ, to give you wisdom to see clearly
and really understand who Christ is and
all that he has done for you.
EPHESIANS 1:16-17 TLB

Faith comes from hearing the Good News, and people hear
the Good News when someone tells them about Christ.
ROMANS 10:17 NCV

[Jesus said] Do not worry about how you will defend
yourselves or what you will say, for the Holy Spirit will teach
you at that time what you should say.
LUKE 12:11-12

. . . I will pray.

Dear Lord,

Among my coworkers, I have become the focus of negative attention since they've discovered that I believe in You. I want to live my life as a believer, but I'm feeling challenged at every turn, being forced to defend my faith. When they pin me down, my words always seem inadequate. My tongue gets tied and my mind shuts down.

In those moments, I pray that Your Holy Spirit would speak through me—in spite of me. I want others to see You clearly when I share Your love and truth. You allow us to represent You, so I pray for the gift of Your calm Spirit and poise under fire as I represent You.

Jesus, You were challenged, too, so this is something You are familiar with. Help me not to take the negativity personally. This is actually a privilege, isn't it—to suffer for You? Today, I will rejoice that I've been placed in the same category as thousands of other believers who have been challenged for their faith across the centuries. I'm not alone or unloved. Please help me to take my eyes off myself.

Amen.

Christianity is the only world religion that is
evangelical in the sense of sharing
good news with others.

Mortimer Jerome Adler

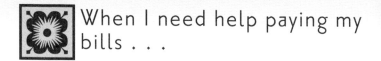# When I need help paying my bills . . .

This same God who takes care of me will supply
all your needs from his glorious riches, which have been
given to us in Christ Jesus.

<small>PHILIPPIANS 4:19 NLT</small>

❀

God is able to make all grace (every favor and earthly
blessing) come to you in abundance, so that you may
always and under all circumstances and whatever the need be
self-sufficient [possessing enough to require no aid or support
and furnished in abundance for every good work
and charitable donation].

<small>2 CORINTHIANS 9:8 AMP</small>

❀

A slack hand causes poverty,
but the hand of the diligent makes rich.

<small>PROVERBS 10:4 RSV</small>

❀

You shall remember the LORD your God, for it is he who
gives you power to get wealth; that he may confirm his
covenant which he swore to your fathers, as at this day.

<small>DEUTERONOMY 8:18 RSV</small>

. . . I will pray.

My Provider,

It's that time of the month again—time to pay my bills. Right now I'm feeling discouraged and nervous, wondering where the money will come from. I really need Your help.

You promise to provide all that I need, so maybe there are things in my life that aren't needs but wants. Please give me the discernment to know the difference. Remind me of all that You've created and all that You own to help me remember that I'm a child of the King of kings—royalty! By Your riches in glory, my needs are met.

Throughout history, You have encouraged Your children by showering them with promises and miraculous rescues when they're in trouble. These financial problems weigh so heavily on my shoulders, but they are light on Yours. Here they are, Lord, with all the concerns attached.

Please calm my nervous heart and help me to remember Your work in past generations. Instead of letting the pile of bills determine my mood, I'll leave them all with You and wait to see how You will work out the provision that I need. Thank You for this opportunity to witness Your power.

Amen.

Cheer up: birds have bills too,
but they keep on singing.

Author Unknown

When I'm overwhelmed by cares . . .

[Jesus said] Come to Me, all who are weary and heavy-
laden, and I will give you rest. Take My yoke upon you and
learn from Me, for I am gentle and humble in heart, and you
will find rest for your souls. For My yoke is easy and My
burden is light.
MATTHEW 11:28-30 NASB

When the cares of my heart are many,
thy consolations cheer my soul.
PSALM 94:19 RSV

[Jesus said] The cares of the world . . . enter in and
choke the word, and it proves unfruitful. But those that were
sown upon the good soil are the ones who hear the word
and accept it and bear fruit.
MARK 4:19-20 RSV

Cast your cares on the LORD
and he will sustain you;
he will never let the righteous fall.
PSALM 55:22

. . . I will pray.

Dear Father God,

The pressures of this life seem to be all around me today—financial and health concerns, worries about my family, concern about the future of our nation. Some days I can keep it all in perspective and push away the care, but other days I feel as if I'm carrying a heavy sack on my back.

I'm not even sure how I should pray for many of these circumstances, so I simply invite You into each situation and ask that You bathe all of them with Your presence and Your influence. When my burdens seem heavier than I can carry, I hand them over to You. On my frame, they simply weigh me down, but You are great enough to hold them all. Help me change my thinking in each of these circumstances.

You may or may not solve every one of these problems, but I pray that You will transform the cares into something light and manageable. Often the greatest way that we come to know You better is through our burdens, so thank You for the privilege of growing to know You more intimately through these cares.

Amen.

He that takes his cares on himself loads himself in vain
with an uneasy burden. I will cast my cares on God;
He has bidden me; they cannot burden Him.

Joseph Hall

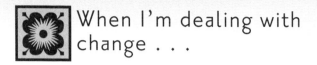

When I'm dealing with change . . .

I am the LORD, I change not.
MALACHI 3:6 KJV

✤

[Moses said] The LORD himself will go before you.
He will be with you; he will not leave you or forget you.
Don't be afraid and don't worry.
DEUTERONOMY 31:8 NCV

✤

[God said]
I'll go ahead of you,
clearing and paving the road.
ISAIAH 45:2 MSG

✤

[The Lord says]
Do not remember the former things,
Nor consider the things of old.
Behold, I will do a new thing,
Now it shall spring forth;
Shall you not know it?
I will even make a road in the wilderness
And rivers in the desert.
ISAIAH 43:18-19 NKJV

. . . I will pray.

Dear Heavenly Father,

A few months ago, my life felt so normal and safe, but suddenly everything is upside down with change. My surroundings were familiar. The people and relationships in my life were steady. My career was headed in a predictable path. Suddenly everything is in flux. How can so many things flip in such a short period of time?

I guess I'm a creature of habit who is resistant to anything other than the familiar, but nowhere in Your Word do You promise a flat life that is always the same. Just the opposite. The only constants in our lives are change and You.

This I know for sure, that You shower me with the same love and protection no matter how the landscape of life varies. When everything around me is fluctuating, help me to keep my focus on Your steady presence and the reassurance of Your Word. I look to Your holy character and unchanging care for me. Help me to see this as an adventure that will result in a positive outcome.

Thank you for holding me steady and for giving me the gift of variety.

Amen.

If we try to resist loss and change or to hold on
to blessings and joy belonging to a past which must
drop away from us, we postpone all the new blessings
awaiting us on a higher level.

Hannah Hurnard

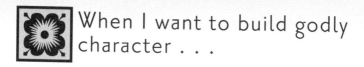

When I want to build godly character . . .

We Christians . . . can be mirrors that brightly reflect the glory of the Lord. And as the Spirit of the Lord works within us, we become more and more like him.

2 CORINTHIANS 3:18 TLB

❧

Do not conform any longer to the pattern of this world, but be transformed by the renewing of your mind. Then you will be able to test and approve what God's will is—his good, pleasing and perfect will.

ROMANS 12:2

❧

We can rejoice, too, when we run into problems and trials for we know that they are good for us—they help us learn to be patient. And patience develops strength of character in us and helps us trust God more each time we use it until finally our hope and faith are strong and steady.

ROMANS 5:3-4 TLB

❧

The character of even a child can be known by the way he acts—whether what he does is pure and right.

PROVERBS 20:11 TLB

. . . I will pray.

Dear Father,

I want to be godly in all the seasons of my life. Help me as I grow older to grow closer to You—to know You better—so that I can become truly a woman made in Your image. Help me to find more time to study Your Word and to become a true imitator of Christ.

Teach me to follow the example of the godly people around me. Many great people whose names may never be known have pleased You by simple obedience and by their love and compassion toward others. Make me like one of them, always putting my own needs aside to serve.

Build in me the kind of stable character that can be trusted. Train me to be a purposeful and bold person who knows what to do and can do it. Give me courage to express what I believe and then to live that way.

Like David, I want to be a person whom people describe as "after God's own heart." So work on me, Father. Make me into the person You created me to become.

Amen.

God has a program of character development for each one of us. He wants others to look at our lives and say, "He walks with God, for he lives like Christ."

Erwin W. Lutzer

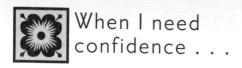

When I need confidence . . .

By awesome deeds in righteousness
You will answer us, O God of our salvation,
You who are the confidence of all the ends of the earth.

PSALM 65:5 NKJV

❁

The LORD will be your confidence,
And will keep your foot from being caught.

PROVERBS 3:26 NKJV

❁

In the fear of the LORD one has strong confidence.

PROVERBS 14:26 RSV

❁

Thus says the Lord GOD, the Holy One of Israel: . . .
"In quietness and confidence shall be your strength."

ISAIAH 30:15 NKJV

❁

When I am afraid, I will put my confidence in you.
Yes, I will trust the promises of God.

PSALM 56:3-4 TLB

. . . I will pray.

Father God,

There are so many opportunities. I want to try everything at once! I want to serve You, Father. I want to be the best person I can be. I want to try new things and succeed at them. Yet my self-confidence needs a boost. I need the courage to go after the dream.

Please help me to look ahead and catch a vision of what You have in store. Give me the confidence to speak up and speak out, to express myself and to stand up for what I believe. Help me realize that in You all things are possible. I can do what You have called me to do and greater things than I imagine because You are with me.

Thank You, Father, for the gift of confidence. Help me to surge ahead and not lag behind when I am unsure of myself. Remind me that I am Your child and that Your Spirit lives and breathes in me—that I can do anything because of that fact. Thank You, Lord.

Amen.

Our confidence in Christ does not make us lazy, negligent, or careless, but, on the contrary, it awakens us, urges us on, and makes us active in living righteous lives and doing good. There is no self-confidence to compare with this.

Ulrich Zwingli

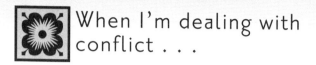

When I'm dealing with conflict . . .

Those who are hot-tempered stir up strife,
but those who are slow to anger calm contention.
PROVERBS 15:18 NRSV

❋

A fool gives full vent to anger,
but the wise quietly holds it back.
PROVERBS 29:11 NRSV

❋

Pursue peace with all people.
HEBREWS 12:14 NKJV

❋

Whoever is slow to anger has great understanding,
but one who has a hasty temper exalts folly.
PROVERBS 14:29 NRSV

❋

A soft answer turns away wrath,
but a harsh word stirs up anger.
PROVERBS 15:1 NRSV

. . . I will pray.

Lord God,

There is much conflict around me just now. Everyone has an opinion. Some personalities seem to naturally collide. Some problems find no resolution. Help me to act as a peacemaker and, in doing so, to find peace myself. Help me to rise above the problems with Your wisdom and guidance and find resolution.

Help me to find peace in the storm, Lord. Remind me that You are in control and that You have good plans for the people involved. Let me see the good in every situation and depend on You to bring that good to the forefront.

Remind me to look to You when I feel overwhelmed. Every day, remind me to seek Your Word on the problems I face. Help me recall what You have taught me and what I know that I might have forgotten. Teach me to hold my tongue and speak only when it will help rather than add to the fray.

Thank You, Father, for a peace that rises above the storm, for the sun shining above the clouds. Thank You for Your presence in my life, a calm assurance that I find in Your answer.

Amen.

To handle yourself, use your head.
To handle others, use your heart.

Donald Laird

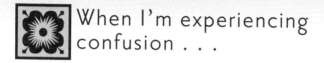

When I'm experiencing confusion . . .

[David said]
You are my lamp, O LORD;
The LORD shall enlighten my darkness.
2 SAMUEL 22:29 NKJV

❋

Let him who walks in the dark,
who has no light,
trust in the name of the LORD
and rely on his God.
ISAIAH 50:10

❋

God is not a God of confusion but of peace.
1 CORINTHIANS 14:33 NASB

❋

Lady Wisdom goes to town, stands in a prominent place,
and invites everyone within sound of her voice:
"Are you confused about life, don't know what's going on?
Come with me, oh come, have dinner with me!"
PROVERBS 9:3-4 MSG

. . . I will pray.

Dear Father,

I am so confused right now. Help me to have a clear view of Your will in my situation. Teach me to trust in You, Lord, for the insight I need.

Train me to think more clearly, to organize well, and to follow Your leading in the decisions I need to make. It is easy to grow smug, thinking my way is best. Show me, Father, and teach me where I can improve.

Help me to find clarity through an understanding of Your ways. Your Word is a light to my path. By it I can be certain of the way and not become confused or frightened. Let that kind of assurance bring peace to my circumstances.

When my mind begins to wander and I get off track from my goals and Your plans, Father, gently lead me back to the best way. Help me to trust in You and not to depend on my own understanding.

You are a guide to the blind and a help to the simple. I praise You for Your strong leadership through the days that I don't see the whole picture. Thank You, Lord, that there's no confusion in You.

Amen.

The greatest moments of your life are those
when through all the confusion God got a message
through to you plain and certain.

Bertha Munro

When I need courage . . .

It is impossible for God to lie. Therefore, we who have fled to him for refuge can take new courage, for we can hold on to his promise with confidence.
HEBREWS 6:18 NLT

✤

[The Lord said] Have I not commanded you? Be strong and courageous. Do not be terrified; do not be discouraged, for the LORD your God will be with you wherever you go.
JOSHUA 1:9

✤

Keep alert, stand firm in your faith, be courageous, be strong.
1 CORINTHIANS 16:13 NRSV

✤

The high and lofty one . . . the Holy One, says this: ". . . I refresh the humble and give new courage to those with repentant hearts."
ISAIAH 57:15 NLT

✤

We are God's household, if we keep up our courage and remain confident in our hope in Christ.
HEBREWS 3:6 NLT

. . . I will pray.

Dear Lord,

So much of the news has been frightening lately. I find myself worried and apprehensive. I know You do not want me to live in fear. Your Word reminds me often that I should "fear not" but "be strong and of good courage."

When I begin to feel alarm rising, bring to my mind the words of comfort that You have given me in Scripture. Teach me to trust completely in Your care not only when the sun is shining and all is well. Give me a new assurance of Your watchful care over me. Stabilize me in that trust so that I will have no doubt that You are there and that You protect me.

Don't let me believe fearmongers with their never-ending stories that plant seeds of fear in my heart. Instead, fill my mind with the truth that You will never leave me nor forsake me.

You have numbered the stars and counted the hairs on my head. You see when a sparrow dies and have assured me that I am much more valuable in Your eyes. Because You are with me, I face life with courage.

Amen.

Have plenty of courage. God is stronger than the devil. We are on the winning side.

John Jay Chapman

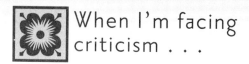 When I'm facing
criticism . . .

*[Jesus said] Blessed are you when people insult you, persecute
you and falsely say all kinds of evil against you because
of me. Rejoice and be glad, because great is your reward
in heaven, for in the same way they persecuted
the prophets who were before you.*
MATTHEW 5:11-12

*Your conversation should be so sensible and logical that
anyone who wants to argue will be ashamed of himself
because there won't be anything to criticize
in anything you say!*
TITUS 2:8 TLB

*Don't speak evil against each other, my dear brothers and
sisters. If you criticize each other and condemn each other,
then you are criticizing and condemning God's law.*
JAMES 4:11 NLT

*We stand true to the Lord whether others honor us or despise
us, whether they criticize us or commend us.*
2 CORINTHIANS 6:8 TLB

. . . I will pray.

Dear Father,

I know that if I obey Your leading, I will be inviting criticism. But Your Word teaches me that when I am mistreated for doing what is right, I am blessed. So I pray for Your blessing, Lord.

Help me to go against the tide when I know that what I'm going to do is good and right. Teach me to be the minister of Your truth and love to those I encounter. Help me to turn away anger with a soft answer and to trust You to protect me when I need protection.

Thank You, Lord, for a chance to serve You. Help me to do it not for any personal benefit but simply in obedience to Your prompting. Whether or not the critics see the value in what I do or ever accept it as a good thing, may I do it anyway. To please You, Lord, is my primary goal.

Help me to have a humble attitude and let my behavior be a testimony of Your work in my life. Give me grace, Father, not to retaliate when criticized, but rather to love the way You do.

Amen.

To avoid criticism, do nothing,
say nothing, be nothing.
Elbert Green Hubbard

When I'm in danger . . .

During danger he will keep me safe in his shelter.
He will hide me in his Holy Tent,
or he will keep me safe on a high mountain.

❁

The LORD is your protection;
you have made God Most High your place of safety.
Nothing bad will happen to you;
no disaster will come to your home.
PSALM 91:9-10 NCV

❁

The LORD will protect you from all dangers;
he will guard your life.
The LORD will guard you as you come and go,
both now and forever.
PSALM 121:7-8 NCV

❁

The Lord will rescue me from every evil attack and
will bring me safely to his heavenly kingdom.
To him be glory for ever and ever. Amen.
2 TIMOTHY 4:18

. . . I will pray.

Dear God,

How many times in my life have You rescued me when I might not have realized it? In the midst of accidents, illnesses, storms, and other dangers, You were there. You are no superhero manufactured by someone's imagination. You are my real, living Hero.

Help me through this hour, too, Lord. I am in danger. I need You. David said that even if he walked through the valley of the shadow of death, he would not fear evil because You were with him. Let those words embolden me.

I am afraid. Help me to lean on You and not on what I can understand. Renew my faith and trust in who You are. Protect me and keep me safe from all harm. I trust in You, Father, for You will never let me down.

There is a scripture that says even a nursing mother might forget her baby, but You will never forget me because I have been carved into Your hand. Thank You for love so strong.

Look at those scars in Your hands and remember me who caused them and come to my rescue, Lord, again, by Your power and strength.

Amen.

Believing God's promises, the Christian is taken through difficulties of every shape and size—and arrives safely.

Richard C. Halverson

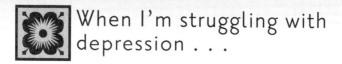# When I'm struggling with depression . . .

My soul melts from heaviness;
Strengthen me according to Your word.
PSALM 119:28 NKJV

❋

The Spirit of the Lord GOD is upon Me, . . .
To console those who mourn in Zion,
To give them beauty for ashes,
The oil of joy for mourning,
The garment of praise for the spirit of heaviness.
ISAIAH 61:1, 3 NKJV

❋

The LORD bless you, and keep you;
The LORD make His face shine on you,
And be gracious to you;
The LORD lift up His countenance on you,
And give you peace.
NUMBERS 6:24-26 NASB

❋

When my anxious thoughts multiply within me,
Your consolations delight my soul.
PSALM 94:19 NASB

. . . I will pray.

Dear Heavenly Father,

Draw me close to You and protect me. I feel the waves of depression sweeping over me. Lord, I can handle this only with Your help. You give the gift of a sound mind and a merry heart. I need both.

The Bible says I should lift my eyes to the hills from whence comes my help. But when depression weighs heavy on me, I have no strength. David called you "the lifter of [his] head." I can envision a loving father with his fingertips lifting a child's face up so he can speak to him. The child's eyes are downcast, but the father's smile reassures him.

Lift my chin up in Your hand, Lord. Help me to see Your face and know You care for me and will help me. Strengthen my faith in You. Strengthen my resolve when the fog and darkness threaten to overwhelm me. Help me to smile again, and renew my hope. Restore laughter and joy to my life.

Thank You for Your promise to be with me always. What other friend cares so much for me, Lord?

Amen.

When you come to the bottom, you find God.

Neville Talbot

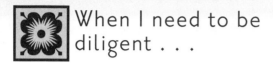

When I need to be diligent . . .

The diligent obtain precious wealth.

PROVERBS 12:27 NRSV

❋

Lazy men are soon poor; hard workers get rich.

PROVERBS 10:4 TLB

❋

The diligent find freedom in their work;
the lazy are oppressed by work.

PROVERBS 12:24 MSG

❋

Easy come, easy go,
but steady diligence pays off.

PROVERBS 13:11 MSG

❋

The path of lazy people is overgrown with briers;
the diligent walk down a smooth road.

PROVERBS 15:19 MSG

. . . I will pray.

Dear Father,

Here I am—no closer to meeting my goals. There are times when it feels as if I'm not making any progress at all, and I know it's my fault. I lack motivation and procrastinate, even on important projects. Lord, help me get going!

Time slips by quickly. One day turns into the next and the next, and before I know it, a week has passed, or a month, or a year and I've accomplished nothing. I need Your help to plan and execute something worthwhile for each day. Faithfulness in a smaller daily task will help me stay focused.

Thank You for letting me know that You have plans for my future. Teach me to be diligent in working toward those plans—excited by what each day may hold.

As I move forward, Lord, keep me going at a steady pace. Help me to begin afresh daily, to challenge myself to accomplish more, to be industrious and hardworking. You have great things ahead for me, and I don't want to miss any of them—not even one!

Amen.

No one ever attains very eminent success by simply doing what is required of him; it is the amount and excellence of what is over and above the required that determines the greatness of ultimate distinction.

Charles Kendall Adams

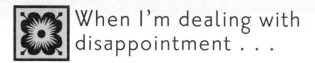 When I'm dealing with
disappointment . . .

*I am still not all I should be, but I am focusing all my
energies on this one thing: Forgetting the past and looking
forward to what lies ahead, I strain to reach the end of the
race and receive the prize for which God, through Christ
Jesus, is calling us up to heaven.*
PHILIPPIANS 3:13-14 NLT

We get knocked down, but we get up again and keep going.
2 CORINTHIANS 4:9 TLB

*Why am I so sad?
Why am I so upset?
I should put my hope in God
and keep praising him,
my Savior and my God.*
PSALM 42:11 NCV

*Lord, let your constant love surround us,
for our hopes are in you alone.*
PSALM 33:22 TLB

. . . I will pray.

Dear God,

I wanted so much for my plans to work out, but they didn't. I still believe You want me to dream big, but this is life. Things don't always turn out the way I hope they will. Now I have to let go and move on.

Father, thank You for caring about my dreams. I know you do. You don't like to see me disappointed. But I also know You have better plans—wonderful plans for my life that will not fall through. The plans You have for me will someday be reality. In fact, they already are reality because when You speak, things happen.

Help me remember when I begin to feel sorry for myself that Your plans are much better than my own. Mine are always flawed by my own limited thinking, lack of understanding, and misconceptions about myself. You see things so much better, so much clearer. Give me patience and stamina to wait for the right plan—the one You have conceived for me.

In the meantime, Lord, help me to have a good attitude. Keep me growing into a godly woman. My reactions to disappointments like this one will show everyone, including me, how far I have come. Thank You for the chance to grow.

Amen.

Faith is often strengthened right at the place of disappointment.

Rodney McBride

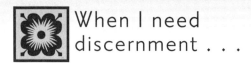

When I need discernment . . .

The discerning heart seeks knowledge,
but the mouth of a fool feeds on folly.
PROVERBS 15:14

❀

Test everything. Hold on to the good.
1 THESSALONIANS 5:21

❀

Solid food is for the mature, for those whose faculties have
been trained by practice to distinguish good from evil.
HEBREWS 5:14 NRSV

❀

The word of God is living and active, sharper than any two-
edged sword, piercing to the division of soul and spirit, of
joints and marrow, and discerning the thoughts and intentions
of the heart.
HEBREWS 4:12 RSV

❀

On the lips of the discerning, wisdom is found.
PROVERBS 10:13 NASB

. . . I will pray.

Dear Father,

I'll be honest—I don't know what to do in this situation. My natural intuition can be misleading, and it doesn't matter anyway because I want to be dependent on You, Father—not on feelings. How can I know that I am making the right decision? How can I know that I'm staying on track with Your plan for me?

Give me eyes to see things as Solomon did—to catch the nuances and the telling details that should guide me to do the right thing. Make me able to decipher the truth. Show me through Your Word, Lord, what I should do. Show me when I'm about to take a misstep and when I need to tread lightly and carefully.

Give me courage to use what You reveal to me in a productive way. Thank You for the truth and for being the light that helps me see it clearly. I never walk alone when I have You by my side to show me the way. Knowing that, submitting to it, treasuring it, makes me stronger, wiser, and more confident. Thank You, Lord.

Amen.

A moment's insight is sometimes worth
a life's experience.

Oliver Wendell Holmes

.

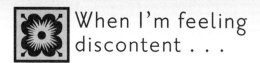

When I'm feeling discontent . . .

[Jesus said] You're blessed when you're content with just who you are—no more, no less. That's the moment you find yourselves proud owners of everything that can't be bought.

Matthew 5:5 msg

❁

[Jesus said] If you're content to simply be yourself, your life will count for plenty.

Matthew 23:12 msg

❁

I have learned to be content in whatever circumstances I am.

Philippians 4:11 nasb

❁

Godliness with contentment is great gain.

1 Timothy 6:6

❁

As for me, my contentment is not in wealth but in seeing you [Lord] and knowing all is well between us. And when I awake in heaven, I will be fully satisfied, for I will see you face to face.

Psalm 17:15 tlb

. . . I will pray.

Dear Lord,

I'm down in the dumps. Forgive me for letting myself become so discontent. I know it is when I compare myself with others that I fall into this trap. I start wanting what others have and complaining about my lot in life. They have more and better. They have easier jobs, a nicer home. They are better-looking, smarter, and thinner. O Father, forgive me and help me to adopt a better attitude!

The comparison game has become such a habit, and it is keeping me from enjoying my life. I need Your help to change. Help me to take my eyes off myself and to love others enough to rejoice with them when You shower them with blessings. When one member of the body of Christ is blessed, we all are. So today, when I see good things happening for others, I will rejoice. When the good things come my way, I will rejoice. I'm determined to develop a thankful and contented heart.

O Father, thank You for Your goodness to me. How could I ever complain? You have blessed me beyond measure. Thank You for having patience with me.

Amen.

Contentment is not the fulfillment of what you want,
but the realization of how much you already have.
Author Unknown

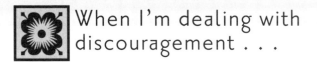

When I'm dealing with discouragement . . .

Let all who are discouraged take heart.
Let us praise the Lord together, and exalt his name.
PSALM 34:2-3 TLB

O my soul, don't be discouraged. Don't be upset.
Expect God to act! For I know that I shall again have plenty
of reason to praise him for all that he will do.
He is my help! He is my God!
PSALM 42:11 TLB

Be encouraged, you who worship God.
The LORD listens to those in need.
PSALM 69:32-33 NCV

When I pray, you answer me;
you encourage me by giving me the strength I need.
PSALM 138:3 NLT

I would have despaired unless I had believed that
I would see the goodness of the LORD
In the land of the living.
PSALM 27:13 NASB

. . . I will pray.

Dear Lord,

I'm trying to put my feelings aside and get busy, but it's tough today. I feel such a sense of discouragement. I've been working so hard, and now I'm not sure if any of my efforts will make any difference at all. On the surface at least, this situation seems hopeless.

The crazy thing is that I know better. I've seen You move and change and intervene in many seemingly hopeless causes, and You never fail to turn them around. So I know I just need to keep going, keep moving, keep on keeping on until I see Your mighty hand pulling everything together. But until then, Lord, I could use some encouragement—a little lift. Help me to look up instead of down and forward instead of backward. Transform my discouraged heart into a vessel that is prepared to celebrate the victory.

Thank You, Lord, for being the sunshine in my life. Right now, I ask You to chase away the shadow of discouragement and send me away with renewed hope.

Amen.

Should we feel at times disheartened and discouraged, a confiding thought, a simple movement of heart toward God will renew our powers. Whatever He may demand of us, He will give us at the moment the strength and the courage that we need.

François Fénelon

When I'm experiencing the pain of divorce . . .

He heals the brokenhearted,
binding up their wounds.

PSALM 147:3 TLB

"Don't be afraid, because you will not be ashamed.
Don't be embarrassed, because you will not be disgraced.
You will forget the shame you felt earlier; you will not
remember the shame you felt when you lost your husband.
The God who made you is like your husband. His name is
the LORD All-Powerful. The Holy One of Israel is the one
who saves you. He is called the God of all the earth.
You were like a woman whose husband left her, and you were
very sad. You were like a wife who married young and then
her husband left her. But the LORD called you to be his,"
says your God.

ISAIAH 54:4-6 NCV

I am overcome with joy because of your unfailing love,
for you have seen my troubles,
and you care about the anguish of my soul.

PSALM 31:7 NLT

. . . I will pray.

Dear Father,

The divorce has left big cracks in my heart and giant-sized holes in my self-esteem. If I didn't have You in my life, there would be no hope. But it is You, Lord, who comes to me at my weakest hours. It is You who comes to embrace me and heal my wounds. Thank You for the knowledge that You are near.

People will fail, and I have failed myself, but You are amazing—always there—always listening—always caring. I guess that's what "amazing grace" means.

You have always been good to me, God. You found me and came to me when I was too pained to come looking for You, and You will not turn Your back and walk away. You are my Help, my Guide, and my Counselor. I need You so much.

Help me to keep my heart right toward You, Lord, and toward others, especially my former husband. Help me not to become bitter but to freely forgive as You have forgiven me. Use this experience to make me a better and more compassionate person. With You I know I can get through these days. Thank You for walking with me.

Amen.

How sweet the name of Jesus sounds
In a believer's ear!
It soothes his sorrows, heals his wounds,
And drives away his fear!

John Newton

When I have doubts . . .

[Jesus said] Have faith in God. Truly I tell you, if
you say to this mountain, "Be taken up and thrown into the
sea," and if you do not doubt in your heart, but believe that
what you say will come to pass, it will be done for you. So I
tell you, whatever you ask for in prayer, believe that you have
received it, and it will be yours.

MARK 11:22-24 NRSV

Let your roots grow down into [Christ Jesus] and draw up
nourishment from him, so you will grow in faith, strong and
vigorous in the truth you were taught.

COLOSSIANS 2:7 NLT

[Jesus said] Do not fear, only believe.

MARK 5:36 RSV

*

[Jesus] said to Thomas, "Put your finger here and
see my hands. Reach out your hand and put it in my side.
Do not doubt but believe." Thomas answered him, "My Lord
and my God!" Jesus said to him, "Have you believed because
you have seen me? Blessed are those who have not seen
and yet have come to believe."

JOHN 20:27-29 NRSV

. . . I will pray.

Dear Father,

Hear me today. Are You listening? I am having so much trouble believing just now. The heavens seem hard as lead, and You seem far away. But, Father, I know that even when I doubt, You hear. Even when I cannot see You, You are there. Even when I cannot hear Your voice, You are patiently speaking to my heart.

Take my mustard seed of faith, and develop it into that faith that moves mountains—faith that is worthy of You. Teach me Your Word. Help me to plant the truth in my heart and soul so that I can draw on it in times when doubts plague me. Help me to find more time to meditate on Your Word, to study those men and women who were the heroes of faith. They are my mentors.

Thank You for bearing with me when I have been a doubting Thomas. You have reached Your hands out to me and let me feel my way to knowing. But now, I want to become strong in faith and overcome my doubts until I can believe for anything. Like Abraham, I will be strong in faith, giving glory to You.

Amen.

Every step toward Christ kills a doubt.

Theodore Ledyard Cuyler

When I need endurance . . .

We pray that you'll have the strength to stick it out
over the long haul—not the grim strength of gritting your
teeth but the glory-strength God gives. It is strength that
endures the unendurable and spills over into joy, thanking the
Father who makes us strong enough to take part in everything
bright and beautiful that he has for us.

COLOSSIANS 1:11-12 MSG

The one who endures to the end will be saved.

MATTHEW 10:22 NRSV

[Jesus said] In the good soil, these are the ones who, when
they hear the word, hold it fast in an honest and good heart,
and bear fruit with patient endurance.

LUKE 8:15 NRSV

In our trouble God has comforted us—and this, too, to help
you: to show you from our personal experience how God will
tenderly comfort you when you undergo these same sufferings.
He will give you the strength to endure.

2 CORINTHIANS 1:6-7 TLB

. . . I will pray.

Dear Father,

I find myself in the middle of another long and difficult ordeal. Help me to endure—to hold up through this trying time—to make it through to a resolution. We both know that staying in the game is a challenge for me. My tendency has always been to bail when the going gets tough and let other people pick up the pieces.

I don't want that to happen this time, especially now that I know more about You. I know that nothing is too hard for You, and when I'm weak, Your strength becomes apparent in me.

Like a coach training an athlete, keep me centered on the goal. Remind me of Your promise to be with me when I begin to waver. Each time I begin to faint and falter, lift me up and put me back on track.

With You at my side, I know I won't have to endure this hardship alone. Every step I take, You take right along with me—keeping me on my feet, providing a shoulder for me to lean on. Thank You, Lord, for Your prodding, Your encouragement, and the strength to endure.

Amen.

Nothing great was ever done without
much enduring.

Catherine of Siena

When I'm being harassed by my enemies . . .

[The Lord] delivered me from my strong enemy, from those who hated me—I who was helpless in their hands. On the day when I was weakest, they attacked. But the Lord held me steady. He led me to a place of safety, for he delights in me.

PSALM 18:17-19 TLB

✦

[Jesus said] You have heard that it was said, "You shall love your neighbor and hate your enemy." But I say to you, Love your enemies and pray for those who persecute you, so that you may be sons of your Father who is in heaven.

MATTHEW 5:43-45 RSV

✦

Do not take revenge, my friends, but leave room for God's wrath, for it is written: "It is mine to avenge; I will repay," says the Lord. On the contrary:
"If your enemy is hungry, feed him;
if he is thirsty, give him something to drink.
In doing this, you will heap burning coals on his head."
Do not be overcome by evil, but overcome evil with good.

ROMANS 12:19-21

. . . I will pray.

Dear Father,

I'm not sure why anyone would go to the trouble to be my enemy. It's as if some people don't have lives of their own so they go around harassing others, trying to feel better about themselves. My job isn't to analyze or solve their issues, though, Lord. My job is to make sure that I respond in a healthy and godly way. As always, Lord, I'm going to need Your help with that.

When Jesus walked here on earth, He had a lot to say about how we should deal with our enemies. His teachings sound simplistic—but they aren't. They cut straight across our pride and human nature. When my impulse is to punch back, Jesus says to turn the other cheek. When my human wisdom says to cut that person off for good, Jesus says to forgive. It's tough, but I want to respond in a way that is productive in my life and even in the lives of those who are harassing me. Most of all, I want to do as Jesus did, understanding that overcoming evil with good is pleasing in Your eyes.

Give me grace and love to deal with my enemies, Lord, and protect my heart from becoming bitter as I strive to please You.

Amen.

We should conduct ourselves toward our enemy as if
he were one day to be our friend.

Cardinal John Henry Newman

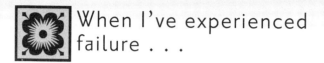# When I've experienced failure . . .

I am waiting for you, O LORD.
You must answer for me, O Lord my God.
I prayed, "Don't let my enemies gloat over me
or rejoice at my downfall."
PSALM 38:15-16 NLT

❀

I let it all out;
I said, "I'll make a clean breast of my failures to GOD."
Suddenly the pressure was gone—
my guilt dissolved,
my sin disappeared.
PSALM 32:5 MSG

❀

You know me inside and out, you hold me together,
you never fail to stand me tall in your presence
so I can look you in the eye.
PSALM 41:12 MSG

❀

And we know that God causes all things
to work together for good to those who love God,
to those who are called according to His purpose.
ROMANS 8:28 NASB

. . . I will pray.

Dear Father,

Some call You "Abba." I've heard it means Daddy. And I need a daddy right now to encourage me. I tried so hard—really thought I had it together—but I flopped, and my self-confidence has taken a beating.

What a relief it is to know that I don't have to worry about Your putting me down or laughing or calling me a loser. You want me to succeed, and You lift me up as a daddy would a fallen child. You dust me off and encourage me to keep trying.

Thank You for Your reassurance, Father. Thank You for showing me that the fact that I failed proves that at least I was trying! I shot for the stars and hit only the ceiling, but I did shoot!

Help me to keep this all in perspective. This failure isn't the end of the world, but I do want to learn from it and succeed next time. Help me to hear Your voice so that I can follow Your leadership and Your timing. Fill me with Your wisdom so that I can do Your will and You can crown my efforts with success.

Amen.

A failure is not someone who has tried and failed;
it is someone who has given up trying and resigned
himself to failure; it is not a condition, but an attitude.

Sydney J. Harris

When I need faith . . .

Faith comes from hearing the message,
and the message is heard through the word of Christ.
ROMANS 10:17

❀

We walk by faith, not by sight.
2 CORINTHIANS 5:7 NASB

❀

Your faith is growing more and more, and the love that every
one of you has for each other is increasing.
2 THESSALONIANS 1:3 NCV

❀

None who have faith in God will ever be
disgraced for trusting him.
PSALM 25:3 TLB

❀

[Jesus said] Anything is possible if you have faith.
The father instantly replied, "I do have faith; oh,
help me to have more!"
MARK 9:23-24 TLB

. . . I will pray.

Dear Lord God,

My faith is small—and my need is so big! Wouldn't it be nice if it were the other way around? And I think I know why. I'd like to say that I'm doing all the things that generate faith, but I'm not—and You already know that. Please forgive me for being so lazy and whiny and self-willed. Big surprise—those qualities eat away at my faith rather than building it up.

Lord, I want to change the faith quotient in my life by doing the things that strengthen faith. Give me a renewed passion for Your Word—the Bible. I believe that as I read from Your powerful letter, the roots of faith will take hold deep down in my soul.

I also want to give myself to prayer—not the whimpering, self-absorbed type of prayer, but making myself a frequent visitor to Your throne on behalf of the needs of others and concerns for the world around me.

Remind me often, Lord, that faith is really just a deepening realization of who You are and how You choose to relate to me. Thank You for being the Rock on which I can anchor my faith.

Amen.

Faith does not mean believing without evidence.
It means believing in realities that go beyond sense
and sight—for which a totally different sort of
evidence is required.

John Baillie

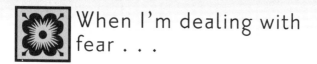

When I'm dealing with fear . . .

I, the LORD your God,
hold your right hand;
it is I who say to you, "Fear not,
I will help you."

ISAIAH 41:13 RSV

❀

God hath not given us the spirit of fear;
but of power, and of love, and of a sound mind.

2 TIMOTHY 1:7 KJV

❀

Fear not, for I am with you,
be not dismayed, for I am your God;
I will strengthen you, I will help you,
I will uphold you with my victorious right hand.

ISAIAH 41:10 RSV

❀

[Jesus said] Peace I leave with you; my peace I give you.
I do not give to you as the world gives. Do not let your hearts
be troubled and do not be afraid.

JOHN 14:27

. . . I will pray.

Dear Father,

Sometimes I'm literally afraid of my own shadow. You've heard the list before—I'm afraid of getting sick, losing someone I love, doing something embarrassing, making a mistake, failing to achieve, becoming a victim of crime—well, as I said, up to and including my shadow!

Lord, I know that these fears greatly limit my ability to live my life to the fullest as You intended. I need Your help, Lord, to double back on fear and conquer it with faith.

Right now, I submit my fears to You as a whole. I identify them as sin—as failure to trust You with those things that are important to me. Forgive me, and help me to establish You as Lord of my life rather than that phony king—fear. And, Father, in the days and weeks ahead, help me to deal with each of my fears one by one, stripping it of its power and chasing it from my life. Thank You, Lord, for helping me to become fearless as I knowingly, determinedly replace my fears with faith in Your goodness.

Amen.

God incarnate is the end of fear; and the heart
that realizes that He is in the midst . . . will be quiet
in the midst of alarm.

F. B. Meyer

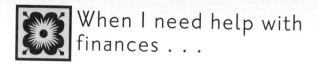

When I need help with finances . . .

Go to the ant . . .
consider its ways, and be wise.
Without having any chief
or officer or ruler,
it prepares its food in summer,
and gathers its sustenance in harvest.

PROVERBS 6:6-8 NRSV

[Jesus said] Whoever can be trusted with very little can also
be trusted with much, and whoever is dishonest with very
little will also be dishonest with much.

LUKE 16:10

The wise have wealth and luxury,
but fools spend whatever they get.

PROVERBS 21:20 NLT

*

She looks over a field and buys it,
then, with money she's put aside, plants a garden.

PROVERBS 31:16 MSG

. . . I will pray.

Dear Lord,

Just when I think I'm getting a little bit ahead, making a little progress with the long-term bills, and even thinking savings could become more than a distant dream, something happens that completely derails us—the refrigerator stops running, the car breaks down, I get laid off or sick or both. And just like that, it all falls apart. This time is no exception.

Lord, I need Your help again. I thought I had all the bases covered this time, but I never could have anticipated this complication. Now, I'm going to have to rearrange everything, set some bills aside, forget about the savings, and find a way to cover this expense.

Lord, You are the Miracle-Worker who took one small boy's lunch—a loaf of bread and a few small fish—blessed it, and distributed it to more than five thousand hungry people. I pray that You would bless my finances as well, then multiply them to meet my needs. I offer You what I have and ask You to do what I cannot—make it more than enough.

Amen.

God demands the tithe, deserves the offerings,
defends the savings, and directs the expenses.

Stephen Olford

When I need to forgive . . .

Get along with each other, and forgive each other.
If someone does wrong to you, forgive that person
because the Lord forgave you.
COLOSSIANS 3:13 NCV

❋

[Jesus said] Judge not, and you will not be judged;
condemn not, and you will not be condemned; forgive,
and you will be forgiven.
LUKE 6:37 RSV

❋

Peter came to [Jesus] and asked, "Lord, how often should I
forgive someone who sins against me? Seven times?"
"No!" Jesus replied, "seventy times seven!"
MATTHEW 18:21-22 NLT

❋

[Jesus said] Whenever you stand praying, forgive, if you have
anything against anyone, so that your Father who is in
heaven will also forgive you your transgressions. But if you
do not forgive, neither will your Father who is in heaven
forgive your transgressions.
MARK 11:25-26 NASB

. . . I will pray.

Dear Good Father,

At first I was shocked, then angry, and now just hurt. I never saw it coming—not at all. But now, like it or not, I've got to deal with it, and that means forgiving. I know it has to be done, but I have to tell You I'll never be able to do it without Your help, Lord.

I ask You first of all to heal my bruised heart. I've tried to "just get over it," but this one went too deep. I release the hurt to You just now. Then, Lord, give me the grace I'll need to forgive the person who wounded me.

I know I may not experience the feeling of forgiveness right away, but I make the objective choice to forgive as an act of my will. I do that with resolve, knowing that You forgave me when I wounded You with my sin and rebellion. I release my offender to Your care, asking that You bless him just as You have blessed me.

Thank You, Lord, for the gift of forgiveness.

Amen.

Humanity is never so beautiful as when praying
for forgiveness or else forgiving another.

Jean Paul Richter

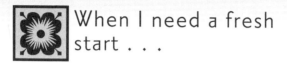

When I need a fresh start . . .

[The Lord says]
Forget the former things;
do not dwell on the past.
See, I am doing a new thing!
Now it springs up;
Do you not perceive it?
I am making a way in the desert
and streams in the wasteland.

ISAIAH 43:18-19

Forgetting what is behind and straining toward what is
ahead, I press on toward the goal to win the prize for which
God has called me heavenward in Christ Jesus.

PHILIPPIANS 3:13-14

GOD made my life complete
when I placed all the pieces before him.
When I got my act together,
he gave me a fresh start.

PSALM 18:20 MSG

. . . I will pray.

Dear God,

Thank You for the seasons. I am always anxious for the change of hot summer to cool autumn, of autumn to cold and restful winter, and again to warm and breezy spring. Each season gives me a fresh perspective on life. Each gives me what I need now, a chance to start over.

I need the spring showers of Your grace to wash me clean and give me a new lease on life. I need the warm, caressing breezes of early summer to gladden my soul and restore my hope. Jeremiah sang of Your mercies being new every morning. Draw me to You early, every day.

Lord, I'm grateful for my salvation—for the opportunity to be washed clean of sin and made worthy to stand in Your presence. I thank You for Jesus who made it all possible through His sacrifice. And I'm glad—so very glad—that my salvation is ongoing. Each day, each hour, each moment, I can reach out to You for a fresh start and You'll be there just waiting for me to ask.

Amen.

If you have made mistakes, even serious mistakes,
there is always another chance for you. . . . You may
have a fresh start any moment you choose, for . . .
"failure" is not the falling down, but the staying down.

Mary Pickford

When I need a friend . . .

Friends love through all kinds of weather.
PROVERBS 17:17 MSG

❋

*Two are better than one, because they have a good reward for
their toil. For if they fall, one will lift up the other.*
ECCLESIASTES 4:9-10 NRSV

❋

*Your friendship was a miracle-wonder,
love far exceeding anything I've known—
or ever hope to know.*
2 SAMUEL 1:26 MSG

❋

As iron sharpens iron, a friend sharpens a friend.
PROVERBS 27:17 NLT

❋

*A man who has friends must himself be friendly,
But there is a friend who sticks closer than a brother.*
PROVERBS 18:24 NKJV

. . . I will pray.

Dear God,

You have always been there for me—always accepting, loving, comforting, meeting my needs. You are the best Friend anyone could ever have. But I believe, Lord, that You are the one who placed this other longing in my heart—the desire for fellowship and friendship with another person.

Believe me, I can see how finding a true friend could be difficult. But I trust that You would not have given me this desire if You didn't already have someone in mind. Maybe it's someone who needs me as much as I need her. I hope so.

Help me to prepare myself by becoming a person who can be trusted, a person who is not self-absorbed and self-serving. Help me to have a cheerful countenance and a friendly spirit. Teach me to be all the things I would want a friend to be.

Keep my heart and mind open, Lord, for the friend You send my way. She may not be like me; she may be so different that she stretches me and helps me grow. She may be different enough to frighten me at first and to surprise me later. I hope so, Lord.

Amen.

A friend is one who knows you as you are, understands where you've been, accepts who you've become, and still, gently invites you to grow.

Author Unknown

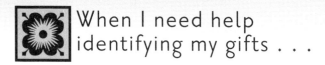# When I need help
identifying my gifts . . .

For we are God's workmanship, created in Christ Jesus to do
good works, which God prepared in advance for us to do.
EPHESIANS 2:10

You created my inmost being; you knit me together in my
mother's womb. I praise you because I am fearfully and
wonderfully made; your works are wonderful,
I know that full well.
PSALM 139:13-14

You created my inmost being; you knit me together in my
mother's womb. I praise you because I am fearfully and
wonderfully made; your works are wonderful,
I know that full well.

Each of us was given grace according to
the measure of Christ's gift. Therefore it is said,
"When he ascended on high he made captivity itself
a captive; he gave gifts to his people."
EPHESIANS 4:7-8 NRSV

And I am convinced and sure of this very thing, that He
Who began a good work in you will continue until the day of
Jesus Christ [right up to the time of His return], developing
[that good work] and perfecting and bringing it to full
completion in you.
PHILIPPIANS 1:6 AMP

. . . I will pray.

Dear God,

Your Word says we all have gifts—unique talents and abilities that were placed within us for Your own plan and purpose. With many people, those gifts are obvious—a rich singing voice, an eye for color, the agile hands of a surgeon, a way with babies. But I feel as if mine are hidden from me. I'm like a curious child on Christmas Eve poking at the red and green gift wrappings covering mysterious packages under the tree. What are my gifts? I feel as if I'm always wondering but never quite discovering.

Reveal them to me, Father. Help me to find what You made me to do best. Show me where I fit into Your plans. What role will I play in the script of life? Help me to get a clear revelation so that I can move out of my timidity and get on with Your purpose and plan, Lord.

Help me in my search, and guide me in my using of those gifts You have imparted to me. I look forward with joy to opening those mysterious packages and sharing them with the world around me.

Amen.

God gives to every man the virtue, temper, understanding, taste, that lifts him into life, and lets him fall just in the niche he was ordained to fill.

William Cowper

When I need help pursuing my goals . . .

Since we are surrounded by such a great cloud of witnesses,
let us throw off everything that hinders and the sin that so
easily entangles, and let us run with perseverance the race
marked out for us. Let us fix our eyes on Jesus,
the author and perfecter of our faith, who for the joy
set before him endured the cross.
HEBREWS 12:1-2

[The Lord said] Record the vision
And inscribe it on tablets,
That the one who reads it may run.
For the vision is yet for the appointed time;
It hastens toward the goal and it will not fail.
HABAKKUK 2:2-3 NASB

You know that in a race all the runners run, but only one gets
the prize. So run to win! All those who compete in the games
use self-control so they can win a crown. That crown is an
earthly thing that lasts only a short time, but our crown will
never be destroyed. So I do not run without a goal.
1 CORINTHIANS 9:24-26 NCV

. . . I will pray.

Dear Father,

I have set goals in my life, but I'm afraid that I will not be able to follow through. Everyday life throws me curves. There are things that interfere, and too readily, excuses present themselves. I have so many responsibilities, so many hats to wear, so many roles to fill, I fear that some of those goals, however important, may never be realized.

Help me to stay focused, Lord. Help me to have a steady focus not only on the end goal, but on the steps and the processes I need to go through to get there. Give me ingenuity to work toward my target when I encounter roadblocks and detours. Give me patience to keep on until the job is done.

When I feel confused or overwhelmed, Father, give me fresh courage to reach for those dreams. Thank You for the motivation that You are to me. My aspirations are a gift from You in the first place. It was You who planted them in my heart, and with Your help I know I can fulfill the plans and reach the goals I have set.

Thank You, Lord, for encouraging me to grow.

Amen.

A written-down goal, in some way no one yet understands, tends to attract every ingredient it needs to realize it.

Author Unknown

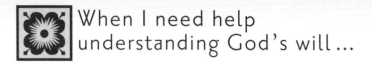

When I need help understanding God's will...

[Jesus said] Anyone who does God's will is my brother, and my sister, and my mother.

MARK 3:35 TLB

[Not in your own strength] for it is God Who is all the while effectually at work in you [energizing and creating in you the power and desire], both to will and to work for His good pleasure and satisfaction and delight.

PHILIPPIANS 2:13 AMP

As your plan unfolds, even the simple can understand it.

PSALM 119:130 TLB

David said, "All these plans were written with the LORD guiding me. He helped me understand everything in the plans."

1 CHRONICLES 28:19 NCV

"I know what I am planning for you," says the LORD. "I have good plans for you, not plans to hurt you. I will give you hope and a good future."

JEREMIAH 29:11 NCV

. . . I will pray.

Dear Lord,

All my life, I have sought Your will and none other. I have waited—listening for Your voice, looking intently for the pieces of the puzzle, preparing myself for the day when You would launch me into my calling. And still, I continue to wait.

I wonder if You've forgotten me, Lord. Have I missed Your tender call? Have I overlooked Your plan and purpose? No revelation of Your will has opened to me. Or has it?

Is it possible that Your will for my life is not intended to be found in the bold and dramatic but rather in the simple and everyday? Perhaps Your will has been unfolding so quietly, so unobtrusively, that I've pigeonholed it as little more than a passionate interest. Perhaps I've mistakenly believed that Your will for me is somehow unconnected to the life You've given me to live.

Lord, I vow to look around me with fresh perspective, and I ask that You open my eyes to see what I haven't seen before—Your perfect will and purpose for me.

Amen.

Be simple; take our Lord's hand and
walk through things.

Father Andrew

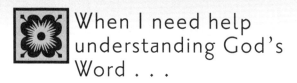

When I need help understanding God's Word . . .

If you want better insight and discernment, and are searching for them as you would for lost money or hidden treasure, then wisdom will be given you, and knowledge of God himself; you will soon learn the importance of reverence for the Lord and of trusting him. For the Lord grants wisdom! His every word is a treasure of knowledge and understanding.

PROVERBS 2:3-6 TLB

Lead me in Your truth and teach me.

PSALM 25:5 NASB

Wisdom begins with respect for the LORD;
those who obey his orders have good understanding.

PSALM 111:10 NCV

Open my eyes, that I may behold
Wonderful things from Your law. . . .
Give me understanding, that I may observe Your law
And keep it with all my heart.

PSALM 119:18, 34 NASB

. . . I will pray.

Dear Father,

Sometimes Your Word can be crystal clear, other times strangely mysterious. Then there are times when I come across a passage that appears to be completely inscrutable. I read it over and over and still can't seem to understand what You are saying to me.

Lord, I wonder when that happens if my human mind is creating barriers to my spiritual understanding. Perhaps I'm trying to apply flawed or inadequate logic to concepts that transcend logical thought. Or I wonder if I cannot break through because of a preconceived assumption or mind-set. Whatever the case, I want to remove any obstacles that keep me from knowing You as You are revealed in the Scriptures. Open my eyes to see and my heart to understand.

I know that Your Word says the Holy Spirit will serve as my Teacher. I invite Him to open my heart and mind to truth, cleanse me from wrong thinking, and make me spiritually minded—one who is capable of rightly grasping spiritual truth. For that, I will give You my greatest respect and devotion.

Amen.

Come, Holy Ghost, for moved by thee
The prophets wrote and spoke;
Unlock the truth, thyself the key,
Unseal the sacred book.

John Calvin

 # When I'm experiencing grief . . .

[Jesus said] Truly, truly, I say to you,
that you will weep and lament, but the world will rejoice;
you will grieve, but your grief will be turned into joy.

JOHN 16:20 NASB

[The Lord] was despised and rejected by men;
a man of sorrows, and acquainted with grief. . . .
Surely he has borne our griefs
and carried our sorrows.

ISAIAH 53:3-4 RSV

I say, "It is my grief
that the right hand of the Most High has changed."
I will call to mind the deeds of the LORD;
yea, I will remember thy wonders of old.
I will meditate on all thy work,
and muse on thy mighty deeds.

PSALM 77:10-12 RSV

🌸

The LORD is near to the brokenhearted
And saves those who are crushed in spirit.

PSALM 34:18 NASB

. . . I will pray.

Dear Lord,

I cry and I cry. I have cried myself out. I can't seem to cry anymore. Help me come to grips with this. Help me to accept what I cannot change. Give me peace and rest. Thank You for being here for me in my time of need. When I find no words, You understand. When I cannot feel anymore, You assure me that I can go on. Thank You for offering Your hand to hold. You are good to me, Lord.

You are helping me to cope. Help me to eventually be able to go beyond coping to healing. Renew my drained emotions. Renew my courage and give me daily support in this battle.

Thank You for friends who bring me comfort, who have held me up in prayer and showed in so many ways that they cared. Those friends come with Your voice, and with Your hands they minister to me.

It is so good to know that You care for me, that You can understand and empathize with the emotions I'm feeling, that each one of my tears is precious to You. Thank You for standing with me, holding me close in this my darkest hour.

Amen.

Grief can be your servant, helping you to feel
more compassion for others who hurt.

Robert Harold Schuller

When I need guidance . . .

Teach me your way, O LORD;
lead me in a straight path.
PSALM 27:11

✤

The LORD will guide you continually,
and satisfy your desire with good things.
ISAIAH 58:11 RSV

✤

The LORD says, "I will guide you along the best
pathway for your life.
I will advise you and watch over you."
PSALM 32:8 NLT

✤

He leadeth me in the paths of righteousness
for his name's sake.
PSALM 23:3 KJV

✤

If you leave God's paths and go astray, you will hear a Voice
behind you say, "No, this is the way; walk here."
ISAIAH 30:21 TLB

. . . I will pray.

Heavenly Father,

Here I am—again—wondering what to do, which way to go. It's not that I'm lost; it's just that I don't know where to go from here. I really do need Your help.

Of course, it would be great if You would just send me some big, impossible-to-miss sign from heaven pointing the way. But I've been here before many times, and I know You typically send Your guidance by less dramatic means—like speaking softly to my heart or through the simple instruction of Your Holy Word.

My part of the transaction is to patiently listen and trust in Your faithfulness. That's a tall order for someone like me—the waiting and listening part, that is. Trusting in Your faithfulness? That's easy. You've never let me down, and I know in my heart of hearts that You never will.

So, show me which way to go, Lord. I'm going to be waiting and listening. That way, I'll hear You—whether it be an impossible-to-miss sign from heaven or a soft whisper deep within my spirit.

Amen.

God is an ever-present Spirit guiding all that
happens to a wise and holy end.

David Hume

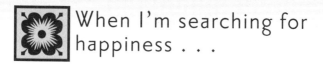# When I'm searching for happiness . . .

LORD, *you have made me happy by what you have done;*
I will sing for joy about what your hands have done.
PSALM 92:4 NCV

❀

You have made known to me the path of life;
you will fill me with joy in your presence,
with eternal pleasures at your right hand.
PSALM 16:11

❀

Taste and see that the LORD is good.
Oh, the joys of those who trust in him!
PSALM 34:8 NLT

❀

Happy are those who trust in the LORD.
PROVERBS 16:20 NRSV

❀

Oh, the joy of drinking deeply from the Fountain of Salvation!
ISAIAH 12:3 TLB

. . . I will pray.

Dear God,

Okay, I've tried everything and looked everywhere. Now I'm asking—no, begging—for Your help to find it. Where is happiness?

I thought happiness would be easy to find but it hasn't been. I see in the distance what looks like happiness, and I think that if I can just be that—or do that—or have that—then I'll be happy. Each time I get near and reach for it, the illusion dissolves before my eyes.

When I think back, with the exception of a few scattered moments of fun, the times when I have truly been happy were moments when I focused on You or did a secret kindness in Your name. Funny thing, but my happiest moments have been when I have forgotten entirely about myself. What I experienced in those moments wasn't mere happiness but something deeper, more soul nourishing and durable. It was joy.

So I'm changing my search, Lord. I'm no longer simply seeking happiness. I'm looking for You. I'm asking for a grateful heart that appreciates Your day-to-day goodness. I'm asking for discerning eyes that see glimpses of You in everyday life. I'm asking You to teach me the secrets of true joy.

Amen.

God cannot give us happiness and peace apart from Himself, because it is not there. There is no such thing.

C. S. Lewis

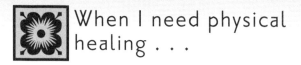

When I need physical healing . . .

I am the LORD who heals you.
EXODUS 15:26 NLT

❉

Pity me, O Lord, for I am weak. Heal me,
for my body is sick.
PSALM 6:2 TLB

❉

Heal me, O LORD, and I shall be healed; save me,
and I shall be saved: for thou art my praise.
JEREMIAH 17:14 KJV

❉

They cried to the LORD in their trouble,
and he saved them from their distress;
he sent out his word and healed them.
PSALM 107:19-20 NRSV

❉

You shall serve the LORD your God, and He will bless
your bread and your water. And I will take sickness
away from the midst of you.
EXODUS 23:25 NKJV

. . . I will pray.

Heavenly Father,

I don't know what's wrong with me. I have things to do, places to go, but my body isn't cooperating. To be honest, I'm a little scared. I'm not used to being sick, unable to make my body do what I want it to. Suddenly, I feel mortal, even frail.

Regardless of how I'm feeling right now, though, I know You are always with me, and one touch of Your healing hands can make me completely whole again. Therefore, Lord, I commit myself to You. I call upon Your love and compassion. I ask You to do for me what I cannot do for myself—heal my body.

If there is something You want to teach me as I wait for Your deliverance, I'm ready to learn it. If there is something I need to hear, a bad habit I need to conquer, let me know. If I've failed to forgive or obey, I'm listening and ready to make it right. Search me, Lord. Know my heart and touch my body.

Thank You, Lord, for being my Healer.

Amen.

No one ever looks in vain to the Great Physician.

F. F. Bosworth

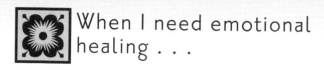

When I need emotional healing . . .

He will wipe away every tear from their eyes;
and there will no longer be any death; there will no longer
be any mourning, or crying, or pain.

REVELATION 21:4 NASB

❁

God blesses those who are kind to the poor. . . . He nurses
them when they are sick, and soothes their pains and worries.

PSALM 41:1,3 TLB

❁

He will not break the bruised reed, nor quench the dimly
burning flame. He will encourage the fainthearted,
those tempted to despair.

ISAIAH 42:3 TLB

❁

Those who discover these words live, really live;
body and soul, they're bursting with health.

PROVERBS 4:22 MSG

❁

See to it that no one comes short of the grace of God;
that no root of bitterness springing up causes trouble,
and by it many be defiled.

HEBREWS 12:15 NASB

. . . I will pray.

Dear Father,

My old "war wounds" are giving me trouble again. You know—injuries on my soul sustained during one of life's many battles. About the time I think they're healed, they start aching again. I examine them, and sure enough, they're inflamed and festering with more hidden shrapnel.

Some of those war wounds are self-inflicted, the result of my own failures. And I feel guilty when I see the disfigurement they've left on my life. And then there are gashes caused by people I've trusted and loved—betrayal, friendly fire that scars the deepest. The rough-and-tumble joust of living has left marks too.

On the outside, I may look healed, but, Lord, You know I'm walking wounded.

It may be a painful process, but I want my soul to be healed and healthy. Great Physician, Mighty Counselor, go over my wounds again, one at a time. Open and drain my memories of their poison. Bring to the surface hidden sins so I can confess them and be forgiven. Remind me of wrongs, and give me courage to make things right. And bitterness and unforgiveness—what deadly toxins! Help me to forgive my enemies as Jesus did His so I can be healed and free.

Restore my wounded heart so it can beat with Your joy.

Amen.

As we practice the work of forgiveness we discover
more and more that forgiveness and healing are one.

Agnes Sanford

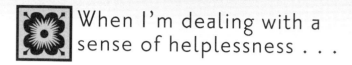

When I'm dealing with a sense of helplessness . . .

GOD takes the side of the helpless;
when I was at the end of my rope, he saved me.
PSALM 116:6 MSG

❈

You have been a defense for the helpless,
A defense for the needy in his distress.
ISAIAH 25:4 NASB

❈

Lord, because I am poor and helpless, please remember me.
You are my helper and savior. My God, do not wait.
PSALM 40:17 NCV

❈

The LORD lifts the poor from the dirt
and takes the helpless from the ashes.
He seats them with princes.
PSALM 113:7-8 NCV

❈

The LORD is my strength and my shield;
My heart trusts in Him, and I am helped;
Therefore my heart exults,
And with my song I shall thank Him.
PSALM 28:7 NASB

. . . I will pray.

Dear Lord,

Any ideas what I should do next, Lord? I'm fresh out of bright schemes and plans. Nothing I've done seems to make the slightest difference, and I can't think of anything else to do.

And I'm not just stumped; I'm exhausted too. I've tried and tried and tried. . . .

But You give strength to the weak. You are the Helper to the helpless. Your arms are my resting place. I'm now at the end of what I know to do—nothing is left but to throw myself into Your embrace and trust You'll hold me tightly.

In the past, I've seen surprising circumstances You have orchestrated when my world was bleak and hope was gone. You gladly give wisdom to fools. You've rescued others and me in life's wild stormy nights. This time, my confidence is totally in You.

Comfort me with Your presence through the terrors of the darkness. Whisper words of Your divine peace that surpass human comprehension. Stick with me, Lord. When the light dawns and I know what to do, I want to enjoy the new day with You.

Amen.

Prayer and helplessness are inseparable. Only he who is helpless can truly pray. Your helplessness is your best prayer. It calls from your heart to the heart of God with greater effect than all your uttered pleas.

Ole Hallesby

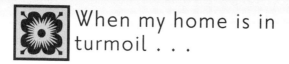
When my home is in turmoil . . .

[God] blesses the home of the righteous.

PROVERBS 3:33 MSG

✿

It takes wisdom to have a good family,
and it takes understanding to make it strong.
It takes knowledge to fill a home
with rare and beautiful treasures.

PROVERBS 24:3-4 NCV

✿

How very good and pleasant it is
when kindred live together in unity! . . .
For there the LORD ordained his blessing, life forevermore.

PSALM 133:1,3 NRSV

✿

If you are pure and live with complete integrity,
he will rise up and restore your happy home.

JOB 8:6 NLT

✿

And above all these [put on] love and enfold yourselves with
the bond of perfectness [which binds everything together
completely in ideal harmony].

COLOSSIANS 3:14 AMP

. . . I will pray.

Lord Jesus,

I know You are making a home for me in heaven with You, but right now, the one I'm living in on earth is in need of serious renovation.

I wish it were only my wood-and-nails house that was a mess. Dust and clutter, by comparison, are easy to clean up. This is a mess of a different sort—emotional chaos and relationships in disarray.

Home should be a resting place, a soft nest where the storms of life can be safely weathered. Right now, my home is under attack from within and without. There are cracks appearing in the walls, and I feel anxious and insecure.

So I ask You, Carpenter of Nazareth, please remake my home. Come and live here now. We need You to be in residence.

Repair the foundations so our trust is firmly placed on You and Your truth. Reinforce our weakened joists and rafters with Your steadfast, patient love. Replace broken, warped windows with wisdom so the light floods in and we can see ourselves clearly. Decorate our home with peace, and furnish it with tender kindness. Mend our roof with willingness and mutual respect.

Amen.

Anyone can build a house;
we need the Lord for the creation of a home.

John Henry Jowett

When I need hope . . .

I would have lost heart, unless I had believed
That I would see the goodness of the LORD
In the land of the living.
PSALM 27:13 NKJV

Why are you cast down, O my soul,
and why are you disquieted within me?
Hope in God; for I shall again praise him,
my help and my God.
PSALM 43:5 RSV

May the God of hope fill you with all joy and peace in
believing, so that you will abound in hope by the power of the
Holy Spirit.
ROMANS 15:13 NASB

Save me from my enemies, GOD—
you're my only hope!
PSALM 143:9 MSG

. . . I will pray.

Dear God,

I just heard a news snippet that makes me question where You are and what You've been doing while evil flourishes. When I hear about bad things—or bad things happen to me—I catch myself wondering. Those thoughts are always followed by the recognition of my own tendency toward foolishness.

You don't bring trouble into our lives—You bring us hope in the midst of the trouble we brought on ourselves. I know Your heart is far more broken over these things than mine is. You are patient and forgiving to evil people—and to me too. You grieve for the wounded as well as those who cause the wounds. So I can't give up hope. If you weren't the Salvager of human souls that You are, the world would have been destroyed long ago.

Though the world around seems dark and hopeless, I want to be like the women who stood before the empty tomb on that first Easter. Their hearts were filled with hope, not because the world had changed, but because their Savior was alive.

Thank You, Lord, for hope enough for my own weary heart and hope enough to share.

Amen.

There is no medicine like hope, no incentive so great,
and no tonic so powerful as expectation
of something tomorrow.

Orison Swett Marden

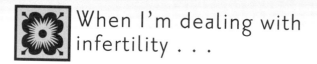

When I'm dealing with infertility . . .

[Hannah] made this vow: "O Lord of heaven, if you will look down upon my sorrow and answer my prayer and give me a son, then I will give him back to you, and he'll be yours for his entire lifetime, and his hair shall never be cut." . . . The Lord remembered her petition; in the process of time, a baby boy was born to her. She named him Samuel (meaning "asked of God") because, as she said, "I asked the Lord for him."

1 SAMUEL 1:11, 19-20 TLB

✣

He gives childless couples a family,
gives them joy as the parents of children.
Hallelujah!

PSALM 113:9 MSG

✣

I trust in you, O LORD;
I say, "You are my God."
My times are in your hands.

PSALM 31:14-15

✣

Delight yourself also in the Lord, and He will give you the desires and secret petitions of your heart.

PSALM 37:4 AMP

. . . I will pray.

Dear God,

I'm pregnant, Lord. I'm carrying a child in my heart.

I'm built for birthing children—at least my heart is. I feel him or her—it doesn't matter which—kicking my soul so robustly that I can barely breathe because of the pain. And I yearn. This is not a desire like a sweet-tooth craving; it is a longing so deep, so fundamental, so genuine that it's physical. My arms ache to hold my baby. My eyes ache to see him. And my womb feels empty.

I see terrible mothers with unkempt, neglected little children. I hear about mothers abandoning or abusing their babies. I read about children born to parents who don't want them, and I wonder why—why don't I have a baby?

But I trust You. For Your own reasons, You have sent me on this strange adventure to bring my baby home. Maybe I'll find my child in a foster home or a foreign land. Perhaps I'll wake up some morning and the pregnancy test will read "positive." Right now, You are preparing my heart to receive the child You have for me.

And if for some divine reason of Your own, a baby never comes, I will trust You in that too.

Amen.

God will either give you what you ask,
or something far better.

Robert Murray McCheyne

When I need a job . . .

Let the thief no longer steal, but rather let him labor,
doing honest work with his hands, so that he may be
able to give to those in need.

EPHESIANS 4:28 RSV

❀

That every man who eats and drinks sees good
in all his labor—it is the gift of God.

ECCLESIASTES 3:13 NASB

❀

You will eat the fruit of your labor;
blessings and prosperity will be yours.

PSALM 128:2

❀

It is good and fitting for one to eat and drink, and to enjoy
the good of all his labor in which he toils under the sun all the
days of his life which God gives him; for it is his heritage. As
for every man to whom God has given riches and wealth, and
given him power to eat of it, to receive his heritage and rejoice
in his labor—this is the gift of God.

ECCLESIASTES 5:18-19 NKJV

. . . I will pray.

Dear God,

Unemployed—that's me. You know it's not my choice, but it's a fact in my life. I'm going to be filling out applications, making calls, checking out leads, knocking on the door of opportunity—and I really need Your advice and assistance.

Here's my situation, Lord: I have bills and financial obligations. Everybody does, but I am responsible only for mine. And I do so want to be responsible. I need to put some money away for the future. I also want to monetarily support worthy programs. I need a job to do these things.

You know the kind of job that would be a good fit for me. You made me a unique person. You put talents in me to be used, and I want to use them.

For these reasons, I need Your guidance. Show me where to go, and teach me what to say. If I need more training or schooling to get the right job, please lead the way. Help me to present myself honestly and confidently to future employers. In the meantime, please provide for my financial needs.

Thank You , Lord, for caring about every aspect of my life— and even more than just caring, acting on my behalf.

Amen.

Each individual has his own kind of living assigned to him by the Lord as a sort of sentry post.

John Calvin

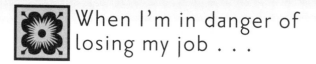 # When I'm in danger of losing my job . . .

They are not afraid of evil tidings;
their hearts are firm, secure in the LORD.
Their hearts are steady, they will not be afraid.
PSALM 112:7-8 NRSV

I have set the LORD always before me;
Because He is at my right hand I shall not be moved.
Therefore my heart is glad, and my glory rejoices;
My flesh also will rest in hope.
PSALM 16:8-9 NKJV

"I know the plans that I have for you," declares the LORD,
"plans for welfare and not for calamity to give you a future
and a hope."
JEREMIAH 29:11 NASB

You will keep in perfect peace all who trust in you,
whose thoughts are fixed on you!
ISAIAH 26:3 NLT

. . . I will pray.

Lord God,

I'm nervous. There are all kinds of rumors. Some are probably only workplace gossip, but if a few of them are true, I may be losing this job and looking for a new one.

Change is always hard, but it's especially difficult when it's unwelcome. It makes me feel frightened and out of control. It brings to mind a host of questions: How will I support myself and take care of my bills? What will a termination do to my career? Where will I find another job?

I'm tense and nervous, but You are the God who speaks peace to troubled souls. I am frightened, but You are the one who says, "Fear not!" because You know all about the future. You will be on the job and busy doing Your work even if tomorrow brings change to mine.

You put people in positions and remove them according to what is best. You open doors of opportunities. I know no matter what happens tomorrow, You will be ready to show me where to go from here. You are a great God who can be completely trusted to meet my needs—job or no job.

Amen.

If God maintains sun and planets in bright and ordered beauty, He can keep us.

F. B. Meyer

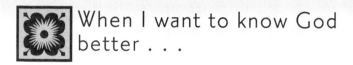 # When I want to know God better . . .

[Jesus said] This is eternal life: [it means] to know (to perceive, recognize, become acquainted with, and understand) You, the only true and real God, and [likewise] to know Him, Jesus [as the] Christ (the Anointed One, the Messiah), Whom You have sent.

JOHN 17:3 AMP

In the past you did not know God. You were slaves to gods that were not real. But now you know the true God. Really, it is God who knows you.

GALATIANS 4:8-9 NCV

I want to know Christ and the power of his resurrection and the fellowship of sharing in his sufferings, becoming like him in his death, and so, somehow, to attain to the resurrection from the dead.

PHILIPPIANS 3:10-11

This is how we may discern [daily, by experience] that we are coming to know Him [to perceive, recognize, understand, and become better acquainted with Him]: if we keep (bear in mind, observe, practice) His teachings (precepts, commandments).

1 JOHN 2:3 AMP

. . . I will pray.

Father God,

I'd like to introduce myself. My name is—how silly is that? You know who I am even better than I do! You've known all about me since I was in my mother's womb—You created me in secret places. It's not You who need to know me better, but I who need and desire to know You better, Lord.

How much better? I want to know Your heart—not just the things You do and say but why You do and say them. I want to know and gain a feel for Your priorities and heartfelt passions. I want to be to You what You have always been to me—a loving friend.

Lord, I plan to apply myself to the study of the Scriptures with renewed dedication. As I do, I pray that You would illuminate my understanding and make Yourself known to me in ways I've never even dreamed about.

My spirit is at home when I am close to You, Lord. I want—with all my heart—to be closer still.

Amen.

Oh, the fullness, pleasure, sheer excitement
of knowing God on Earth!

Jim Elliot

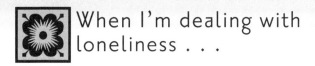

When I'm dealing with loneliness . . .

Even though I walk
through the valley of the shadow of death,
I will fear no evil, for you are with me.

PSALM 23:4

❀

I am continually with You;
You have taken hold of my right hand.

PSALM 73:23 NASB

❀

[Jesus said] I am with you always, to the close of the age.

MATTHEW 28:20 RSV

❀

I meditate on You in the night watches. . . .
My soul follows close behind You;
Your right hand upholds me.

PSALM 63:6, 8 NKJV

❀

How precious are your thoughts about me, O God!
They are innumerable! I can't even count them;
they outnumber the grains of sand!
And when I wake up in the morning, you are still with me!

PSALM 139:17-18 NLT

. . . I will pray.

Father God,

It isn't anyone's fault; it's just the way things worked out—but here I am, alone and feeling lonely. All the comfortable people in my life are far away and out of my reach. I miss them. I'm so grateful, Lord, that You are always here with me, always available, always accepting, loving, comforting, and watching over me. Because of You, I'm never really alone.

Father, I ask that You would be especially present in my life right now. Allow me to feel Your presence around me, wrapping me up like a warm blanket. And thanks in advance for listening to me whenever I have the need to talk to You.

Rather than spending this time longing for those who can't be with me, help me to see this time as an opportunity to draw closer to You. And it may be a time for someone new in my life—a friend I haven't met yet. If so, bring us together, Lord. Open my heart to her and allow me to be the answer to her prayer, just as she is to mine. Thanks for being the one I can always count on.

Amen.

In every man there is a loneliness, an inner chamber of peculiar life into which God only can enter.

George MacDonald

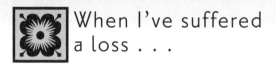 When I've suffered
a loss . . .

*Blessed be the God and Father of our Lord Jesus Christ,
the Father of mercies and God of all comfort, who comforts us
in all our tribulation, that we may be able to comfort those
who are in any trouble, with the comfort with which we
ourselves are comforted by God.*
2 CORINTHIANS 1:3-4 NKJV

*You, O God, do see trouble and grief;
you consider it to take it in hand.*
PSALM 10:14

*This is my comfort in my affliction,
That Your word has revived me. . . .
I have remembered Your ordinances from of old, O LORD,
And comfort myself.*
PSALM 119:50, 52 NASB

*Comfort me with your love,
as you promised me, your servant.*
PSALM 119:76 NCV

. . . I will pray.

Dear Lord,

Gone. Vanished. It disappeared in an instant, and I'm still reeling. On some level, if only intellectually, I've accepted this loss. But like an amputee, I am experiencing phantom pain.

This big gaping hole—what can fill it? Right now, I don't think anything can. I'm tempted to try to fill it with mindless distractions and try to ease the pain with quick pleasures, but those things only cheapen and trivialize my loss.

And I'm tempted to ask You "Why?" But I won't. You could sit down and explain it to me, and it would be like describing nuclear fission to a newborn. So instead, I'll ask You "What?"—What do You want me to put in this hole that my loss has created?

You don't do things haphazardly. You always have a purpose. So tell me, what should I do to cooperate with Your great plan? What do I do next?

I've seen it before: loss can make people bitter. But, Lord, please don't let my loss make me angry and resentful. Let it make me sweeter. Heal me in such a way that the hole in my soul doesn't become an ugly scar but a mark of divinely remade beauty.

Amen.

Our real blessings often appear to us in the shape
of pains, losses and disappointments;
but let us have patience and we soon shall see
them in their proper figures.

Joseph Addison

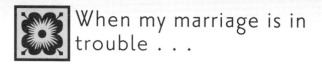# When my marriage is in trouble . . .

Let the husband render to his wife the affection due her,
and likewise also the wife to her husband.
1 CORINTHIANS 7:3 NKJV

*

Better to live alone in a tumbledown shack
than share a mansion with a nagging spouse.
PROVERBS 25:24 MSG

*

They shall be My people, and I will be their God; then I will
give them one heart and one way, that they may fear Me
forever, for the good of them and their children after them.
JEREMIAH 32:38-39 NKJV

*

Submit to one another out of reverence for Christ. Wives,
submit to your husbands as to the Lord. For the husband is
the head of the wife as Christ is the head of the church, his
body, of which he is the Savior. Now as the church submits to
Christ, so also wives should submit to their husbands in
everything. Husbands, love your wives, just as Christ loved
the church and gave himself up for her.
EPHESIANS 5:21-25

. . . I will pray.

Dear God,

"For better or worse"—I remember saying those words. I remember thinking: *We're going to be different. We won't have an "or worse." And if we do, we'll work together. We won't turn on each other.* Well, Father, I now know why they make couples vow to stay together because marriage can be hard—very hard.

Betrayal, hurt, deception, cruelty—I can think of so many reasons to file the paperwork and dissolve our union. It is amazing how many ways two people who once loved each other can find to hurt the other.

Father, I can't do much about all he's done wrong. I'll leave him, his mistakes, and our uncertain future in Your hands. But it takes two to make a marriage and two to break it. So I can do something about my attitude and actions.

Forgive me for the wrongs I have committed, and help me make them right. Give me the grace to swallow my pride and ask him for forgiveness. Adjust my attitude so I am tender, understanding, and forgiving.

Remind us both of the love we shared in the days when we first pledged our love to each other. And help us to be forgiving as You have forgiven us.

Amen.

A good marriage is not one where perfection reigns:
It is a relationship where a healthy perspective
overlooks a multitude of "unresolvables."

James C. Dobson

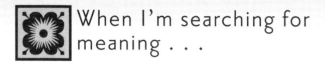 # When I'm searching for meaning . . .

He determined the times set for them and
the exact places where they should live.

ACTS 17:26

Your eyes have seen my unformed substance;
And in Your book were all written
The days that were ordained for me,
When as yet there was not one of them.

PSALM 139:16 NASB

Be strong and steady, always abounding in the Lord's work,
for you know that nothing you do for the Lord is ever wasted.

1 CORINTHIANS 15:58 TLB

We know that in everything God works for good with those
who love him, who are called according to his purpose.

ROMANS 8:28 RSV

. . . I will pray.

Lord God,

Why did You make me? What did You have in mind when You knit me together in my mother's womb? Was there some great and mighty purpose? I hope so—I'd hate to think my only calling in life is to clean, do laundry, cook, follow my boss's instructions, and take care of others.

Even as I speak these words though, I feel ashamed. You have brought a great deal of meaning to my life. You've called me to love You and to be a blessing to the precious people You've placed in my life. Remind my head and my heart that it's a privilege to walk with You each day, to serve You and others. As I fold underwear, mop floors, and do my boss's bidding, confirm that these are more than mundane physical tasks. I'm carrying out an act of love, kindness, and obedience to You.

Father, I thank You for Your grace that enlightens my faulty vision and expands my narrow thinking. Thank You for creating me and giving my life meaning.

Amen.

When people are serving,
life is no longer meaningless.

John W. Gardner

When I need a miracle . . .

LORD God of Israel,
we praise you.
Only you can work miracles.
PSALM 72:18 CEV

How we thank you, Lord! Your mighty miracles
give proof that you care.
PSALM 75:1 TLB

You are the God of miracles and wonders!
You still demonstrate your awesome power.
PSALM 77:14 TLB

Everyone shall stand in awe and confess the greatness of
the miracles of God; at last they will realize what
amazing things he does.
PSALM 64:9 TLB

You are great, and do great miracles. You alone are God.
PSALM 86:10 TLB

. . . I will pray.

Dear Lord,

My situation is desperate. I've done all I know to do, Lord, and it comes down to this: I need a miracle.

I've always loved all those Bible stories where You parted the clouds and stepped onto center stage. But I've noticed that You especially tend to show up when the individuals involved have done everything they can and have no other resources. You help those who can't help themselves. And I am at that point. I think I've done everything humanly possible and now it is up to You. If You don't do something miraculous—I'm not sure what will happen.

Whatever there is still for me to do, Lord, let me know, and I'll be quick to obey. I wait for Your sure and certain hand of mercy in my situation. And, Lord, there is something more I'd like to say: Thanks for giving me the assurance that no matter what happens, You are with me, overseeing my current circumstances, protecting me and my interests. I praise You, Lord, as the Miracle-Worker—the Giver of grace and mercy.

Amen.

A miracle is an event beyond the power of any
known physical law to produce; it is a spiritual
occurrence produced by the power of God,
a marvel, a wonder.

Billy Graham

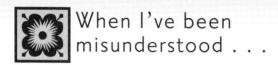When I've been misunderstood . . .

Simeon . . . said to Mary [Jesus'] mother,
"This child [Jesus] . . . [is]
A figure misunderstood and contradicted."
LUKE 2:34 MSG

❉

Vindicate me, O LORD, according to my righteousness
and my integrity that is in me.
PSALM 7:8 NASB

❉

O LORD, You have searched me and known me.
You know when I sit down and when I rise up;
You understand my thought from afar.
You scrutinize my path and my lying down,
And are intimately acquainted with all my ways.
Even before there is a word on my tongue,
Behold, O LORD, You know it all.
PSALM 139:1-4 NASB

❉

Vindicate me in your righteousness, O LORD my God;
do not let them gloat over me.
PSALM 35:24

. . . I will pray.

Dear Lord,

I'm sure glad that You can read my heart and understand my motivations. No one else can. All the others think I'm awful, but they don't have all the facts. If they aren't willing to give me the benefit of the doubt, I don't know how to change their perception.

Lord, this whole situation has stung my heart. It hurts that people I thought knew me could so quickly judge me. All I know to do is to ask You to vindicate me, expose the truth, and help me to heal and forgive.

I know You understand what it's like to be misunderstood, Lord. People disparage You every day, never seeing what You have done for them, how You've sacrificed on their behalf. Instead they blame You for every war and disaster, struggle and loss. My little situation looks pretty lame when I think about it that way. At least now, Lord, I understand in a small, very limited way how You must feel a great deal of the time. And yet, You never let it shake You from Your purpose or keep You from loving and forgiving. Give me a heart like Yours, Lord.

Amen.

Is it so bad, then, to be misunderstood?
Pythagoras was misunderstood, and Socrates, and Jesus, and Luther, and Copernicus, and Galileo, and Newton, and every pure and wise spirit that ever took flesh.
To be great is to be misunderstood.

Ralph Waldo Emerson

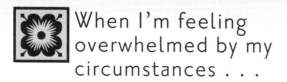# When I'm feeling overwhelmed by my circumstances . . .

From the end of the earth will I cry unto thee, when my heart is overwhelmed: lead me to the rock that is higher than I. For thou hast been a shelter for me, and a strong tower from the enemy. I will abide in thy tabernacle for ever: I will trust in the covert of thy wings.

PSALM 61:2-4 KJV

The ropes of death came around me;
the deadly rivers overwhelmed me.
In my trouble I called to the LORD.
I cried out to my God for help.
From his temple he heard my voice;
my call for help reached his ears.

PSALM 18:4, 6 NCV

Please listen and answer me,
for I am overwhelmed by my troubles. . . .
But I will call on God,
and the LORD will rescue me.

PSALM 55:2, 16 NLT

. . . I will pray.

Dear Lord,

I just don't think I can take anymore. My troubles are piled up like a huge mountain, and I just can't keep climbing. I thought there was a purpose to this and even an end to my grief and suffering—but there doesn't seem to be.

I'm tired, Lord. I don't think I can get through the days ahead. I'm not even sure I can get through this day. Please give me strength to put one foot in front of the next and keep on going. Help me to live one day at a time and not borrow tomorrow's troubles.

Along the way, if I have done things that are wrong, forgive me. Help me to repair the damage I have caused.

I know that You see the future as well as the past. You know how I came to be in these circumstances, and You know the way out—if there is one—so I am willing to trust You, and I want to walk very closely beside You. Please take my hand and help me to navigate through this wilderness. Help me to keep my hope in You as we climb today's mountain.

Amen.

Grace is love that cares and stoops and rescues.

John R. W. Stott

When I'm struggling with my past . . .

Forget the former things;
do not dwell on the past.
See, I am doing a new thing!
Now it springs up; do you not perceive it?
I am making a way in the desert
and streams in the wasteland.

ISAIAH 43:18-19

❀

You will again have compassion on us;
you will tread our sins underfoot
and hurl all our iniquities into the depths of the sea.

MICAH 7:19

❀

With the loving mercy of our God,
a new day from heaven will dawn upon us.
It will shine on those who live in darkness. . . .
It will guide us into the path of peace.

LUKE 1:78-79 NCV

❀

Then I let it all out; I said, "I'll make a clean breast of my
failures to GOD." Suddenly the pressure was gone—
my guilt dissolved, my sin disappeared.

PSALM 32:5 MSG

. . . I will pray.

Heavenly Father,

There are ghosts in my closets—things in my past that haunt me. My mistakes hang around me by day and float over my bed at night, howling, taunting, and terrorizing.

Regrets—there are so many things that I wish I hadn't done, so many times I messed up. I see the damage that my mistakes caused, and I am sorry. I wish I could go back and do things differently. If only I had known then what I know now.

And hurt—I've been hurt by those who should have cared for me. And I've caused hurt. Help me to make these right when I can and release them to You when I cannot.

And forgiveness—I need to forgive. And I need others to forgive me. But first, I need to receive forgiveness from You. Wash me clean from head to foot.

So, Lord—there they are, all the ghosts of my past. I ask that You still their voices and help me to close and lock those closet doors and walk away forever. Help me to find my new life in You.

Amen.

In Christ we can move out of our past into a meaningful present and a breathtaking future.

Erwin W. Lutzer

When I need patience . . .

We continue to shout our praise even when we're hemmed in
with troubles, because we know how troubles can develop
passionate patience in us, and how that patience in turn
forges the tempered steel of virtue, keeping us alert for
whatever God will do next.

ROMANS 5:3-4 MSG

We also pray that you will be strengthened with his glorious
power so that you will have all the patience and endurance
you need.

COLOSSIANS 1:11 NLT

See how the farmer waits for the precious fruit of the earth,
waiting patiently for it until it receives the early and latter
rain. You also be patient.

JAMES 5:7-8 NKJV

We have proved ourselves to be what we claim by our
wholesome lives and by our understanding of the Gospel and
by our patience.

2 CORINTHIANS 6:6 TLB

. . . I will pray.

Father God,

I've had it; I quit! I've done everything I know to do and just look at how things are going. So now it's all up to You.

Okay, maybe it's not fair for me to dump my problems in Your lap when I can't handle them anymore and take them back when I can. I suppose it would be better if I consulted with You on a daily basis and did things Your way all the time. But right now, Lord, I need help. I want You to help me right now!

I'm sorry, Lord. I know I can't order You around. You're God, and I'm not. Please forgive me for being demanding. I've come to the end of myself, and I need Your help.

Help me to be patient in my current circumstances, knowing that there is a time and season for all things. And help me now and in the future not to focus on getting what I want, but to develop the strength of character to be long-suffering and uncomplaining. Show me how to be patient with others as You have been with me.

Amen.

Patience is bitter, but its fruit is sweet.

Jean Jacques Rousseau

When I need peace . . .

To all of you that are in Christ Jesus (the Messiah),
may there be peace (every kind of peace and blessing,
especially peace with God, and freedom from fears,
agitating passions, and moral conflicts).
1 PETER 5:14 AMP

❀

In peace I will both lie down and sleep,
For You alone, O LORD, make me to dwell in safety.
PSALM 4:8 NASB

❀

Embrace peace—don't let it get away!
PSALM 34:14 MSG

❀

I will listen to what God the LORD will say;
he promises peace to his people, his saints.
PSALM 85:8

❀

The LORD blesses his people with peace.
PSALM 29:11

. . . I will pray.

Lord God,

Many disturbing thoughts are plaguing me. I'm panicky and frightened. So many things could go wrong, and any one of them would mean disaster! I know I shouldn't worry, but I can't seem to help it. I'm desperate to shake off this sense of foreboding, Lord, to clear my mind and step out from under this dark, menacing cloud.

In this moment, the one thing I need from You most is peace—the kind that is greater than my understanding, the kind that overrules my current circumstances and my troubled thoughts and brings supernatural calm and comfort. I close my eyes and wait for it here in Your presence. Let Your peace wash over me just now. I surrender to it without reservation.

Thank You, Lord, for making a way to leave confusion and discord behind and for providing a peace that is always accessible as I turn my thoughts to You. Your gift is more than enough, even for my troubled life. I praise You and thank You, my wonderful Prince of Peace.

Amen.

God is a tranquil being and abides in a tranquil eternity. So must your spirit become a tranquil and clear little pool, wherein the serene light of God can be mirrored.

Gerhard Tersteegen

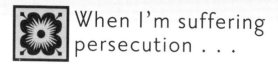

When I'm suffering persecution . . .

Who shall separate us from the love of Christ?
Shall trouble or hardship or persecution or famine or
nakedness or danger or sword?
Romans 8:35

❀

[Jesus said] Remember the word that I said to you,
"A servant is not greater than his master." If they persecuted
me, they will persecute you.
John 15:20 rsv

❀

[Jesus said] Love your enemies, bless them that curse you,
do good to them that hate you, and pray for them which
despitefully use you, and persecute you.
Matthew 5:44 kjv

❀

[Jesus said] You're blessed when your commitment to
God provokes persecution. The persecution drives you even
deeper into God's kingdom.
Matthew 5:10 msg

. . . I will pray.

Precious Lord,

I'm surrounded on all sides, and they're out to get me. I don't entirely understand why they hate me so much, but they do. They are intent on destroying me.

You hear the lies they are spreading about me. You see them plotting my ruin. They think they have backed me into a corner. They don't realize that You are my secret weapon!

Please do not leave me. You are my only safe harbor. You are the only one I can trust. I need You to deliver me from the hands of the cruel and dishonest—from the hands that would persecute me for doing right.

Please don't let me be defeated and humiliated. In the past, You have seen me through trouble and bitter days. I know You will help me again. In the meantime, while this storm continues, my confidence will remain in You. In the midst of this hailstorm of accusations and bullying, I pray that You will change the hearts of my enemies. And I pray that You will strengthen mine.

Amen.

The servant of Christ must never be surprised if he has to drink of the same cup with his Lord.

J. C. Ryle

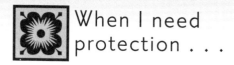# When I need
protection . . .

[God] orders his angels to protect you wherever you go.
<small>PSALM 91:11 TLB</small>

❀

You protect me with salvation-armor;
you hold me up with a firm hand,
caress me with your gentle ways.
<small>PSALM 18:35 MSG</small>

❀

The LORD is my light and the one who saves me.
I fear no one. The LORD protects my life;
I am afraid of no one.
<small>PSALM 27:1 NCV</small>

❀

Deliver me from my enemies, O my God,
protect me from those who rise up against me.
<small>PSALM 59:1 RSV</small>

❀

This I declare of the LORD:
He alone is my refuge, my place of safety;
he is my God, and I am trusting him.
<small>PSALM 91:2 NLT</small>

. . . I will pray.

Father God,

I'm running scared, and I'm running to You for protection.

Look at what surrounds me. I'm trying to be calm and trust in You, but occasionally—like right this very minute—I think about what could happen, and I want to run and hide.

So I will run and hide—in Your arms. You will surround me with Your love. You give the weak strength and the frightened courage—that's me on both counts. When darkness falls, I will rest because You are strong and You are good.

The unknown to me is perfectly clear to You. You see what is going to happen, and I trust that You will lead me away from evil and all harm. Send Your angels to surround me. Plant a fiery hedge of protection around me.

Please look into my heart and soul. If I have brought peril upon myself because of foolishness or wrongdoing, then point out my failures so I can correct them. But in the meantime, be gracious to me and protect me.

Thank You for being trustworthy. Thank You for being strong.

Amen.

Angels are God's secret service agents.
Their assignment—our protection.

Meriwether Williams

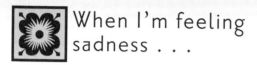 When I'm feeling
sadness . . .

Be kind to me, GOD— . . .
I've cried my eyes out;
I feel hollow inside.
Warm me, your servant, with a smile;
save me because you love me.
PSALM 31:9, 16 MSG

You changed my sorrow into dancing.
You took away my clothes of sadness,
and clothed me in happiness.
PSALM 30:11 NCV

The ransomed of the LORD will return.
They will enter Zion with singing;
everlasting joy will crown their heads.
Gladness and joy will overtake them,
and sorrow and sighing will flee away.
ISAIAH 35:10

. . . I will pray.

Dear Lord,

There are days when the problems that I am carrying chafe my shoulders and weigh me down. Today is one of those days. My heart is lonely, and my soul has lost its courage. The future looks just as bleak as the present. I just don't want to go on.

If I continue to stare at my problems, I know what will happen: My sadness will turn to despair, and that is not what You intend.

But I know, Lord, that as long as You are on the throne, there is no need for gloom. Help me to turn my eyes toward You where the skies are full of promise. Let me see rainbows of hope through my tears. Please, Lord, flood my path with the light of Your Son.

Fill my heart with brave music, and cheer my spirit so I can encourage those who are also burdened. And, Lord, when the day comes to an end, help me to lay my burdens down and rest in confidence that You will carry them—and me—through the night.

Amen.

No one needs to be downcast, for Jesus is the joy of heaven, and it is His joy to enter into sorrowful hearts.

Frederick William Faber

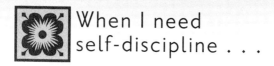

When I need self-discipline . . .

God did not give us a spirit of timidity,
but a spirit of power . . . and of self-discipline.
2 TIMOTHY 1:7

❀

An undisciplined, self-willed life is puny;
an obedient, God-willed life is spacious.
PROVERBS 15:32 MSG

❀

I discipline my body and bring it into subjection,
lest, when I have preached to others, I myself should
become disqualified.
1 CORINTHIANS 9:27 NKJV

❀

Moderation is better than muscle,
self-control better than political power.
PROVERBS 16:32 MSG

❀

[Jesus said] What good is it for a man to gain the whole
world, and yet lose or forfeit his very self?
LUKE 9:25

. . . I will pray.

Dear Lord,

I try not to, but it is so easy to coast into self-indulgence. I don't intend to; I just do. Sometimes indulgence starts with rationalizations: "Tomorrow's another day." "What does it matter if I do it just this once?" "This is the last time."

I know you've heard all my excuses—and apologies. What I need more than anything right now is good old-fashioned discipline, the kind that keeps me on point and moving forward.

I ask that You would be the hand of discipline in my life right now. Nudge me, push me, yank me up short, if necessary. Speak loudly so I can hear Your voice over my excuses. Help me to see those flaws in my character that allow me to indulge my weaknesses. Help me to rid my life of the booby traps I have set for myself.

And as I learn to respond to Your voice without exception—without hesitation—plant Your discipline down deep inside me until I'm able to motivate and chart a productive course for myself. You are my hope for a better life.

Amen.

Self-discipline never means giving up anything,
for giving up is a loss. Our Lord did not ask us to give
up the things of earth, but to exchange them
for better things.

Archbishop Fulton J. Sheen

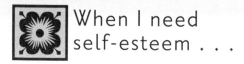

When I need self-esteem . . .

God created people in his own image.
GENESIS 1:27 NLT

[Jesus said] What's the price of a pet canary? Some loose change, right? And God cares what happens to it even more than you do. He pays even greater attention to you, down to the last detail—even numbering the hairs on your head! So don't be intimidated by all this bully talk. You're worth more than a million canaries.
MATTHEW 10:29-31 MSG

Oh yes, you shaped me first inside, then out;
you formed me in my mother's womb.
I thank you, High God—you're breathtaking!
Body and soul, I am marvelously made!
I worship in adoration—what a creation!
PSALM 139:13-14 MSG

[The Lord says] I have engraved you
on the palms of my hands.
ISAIAH 49:16

. . . I will pray.

Lord God,

I am so buffeted by living that I hardly know who I am. I have been insulted, berated, and generally beaten up by life and the people in it. While I am sometimes tempted to join in with the chorus of voices that tell me that I am nothing and nobody, I must not—will not—allow my emotions or passions to seduce me into self-rejection.

We both know I have many faults, but that does not make me worthless. Jesus died for me. He forgives me. No matter what I do or don't do, I'll never be less loved by You. Your Spirit empowers and lives within me.

Although I do not feel it right now, I know I am Your child—precious in Your eyes, beloved by You for all eternity. You hold me safely in Your everlasting embrace.

I am Your own handmade child—a one-of-a-kind original. I am here at this time in history to fulfill Your special purpose. Right now, I need to rest in those truths. Lead me into pastures of inner rest and away from stagnant puddles of meaningless diversion. Restore my soul, and strengthen my self-esteem.

Amen.

A healthy self-image is seeing yourself as God sees you—no more and no less.

Josh McDowell

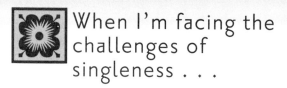# When I'm facing the challenges of singleness . . .

Turn to me and be gracious to me,
for I am lonely.
PSALM 25:16 NRSV

Happy are those who have the God of Israel as their helper,
whose hope is in the LORD their God.
PSALM 146:5 NLT

[God said] I came by again and saw you, saw that you were
ready for love and a lover. I took care of you, dressed you and
protected you. I promised you my love and entered the
covenant of marriage with you. I, GOD, the Master, gave my
word. You became mine.
EZEKIEL 16:8 MSG

Learn to love appropriately. You need to use your head and
test your feelings so that your love is sincere and intelligent.
PHILIPPIANS 1:9-10 MSG

. . . I will pray.

Dear Lord,

Some say, "There's a lid for every pot." Right now, there doesn't seem to be one for me. Some of the time, I'm okay with that. But now and then, in the middle of the night when the house is still, I think, *It would be so nice to hear someone breathing on the other side of the bed.*

Then there are the times when I need a really good hug.

And it would be great to have one other person on earth voluntarily and solely devoted to me—someone I could tell my deepest secrets to—someone I could count on in tough times—someone who would wipe the supper dishes while I wash—a soul mate.

Maybe someday that person will appear. But whether he does or not, I have You. You know my faults and my secrets and love me fully and completely. You have promised never to leave me. You are tender with my vulnerabilities and always kind.

Yes, it's true: every day I am getting older and that clock is ticking off the minutes, hours, and days. But I have confidence that You will be faithful to me always. Dearest Lover of my soul, with You I can be alone and yet not lonely.

Amen.

Christ understands loneliness; He's been through it.

Paul Stromberg Rees

When I can't sleep . . .

I will both lie down in peace, and sleep;
For You alone, O LORD, make me dwell in safety.
PSALM 4:8 NKJV

If you sit down, you will not be afraid;
when you lie down, your sleep will be sweet.
PROVERBS 3:24 RSV

The LORD gives sleep to those he loves.
PSALM 127:2 NCV

The fear of the LORD leads to life,
So that one may sleep satisfied, untouched by evil.
PROVERBS 19:23 NASB

Find rest, O my soul, in God alone;
my hope comes from him.
PSALM 62:5

. . . I will pray.

Dear Father of Light,

We're having a long night—You and I. We've talked over some things in the past that I'm unhappy about and some things that You're unhappy about. (I'm really sorry about those things! Please forgive me!)

And then we've been talking over the future. I can't see around corners the way You can. I can only imagine what's ahead. Once in a while, my imagination paints a rosy picture of tomorrow. More often than not, it conjures up rather gloomy visions. And then there are the imaginings that are simply frightening.

Along with my past mistakes and failures, it is the gloomy and scary visions that seem to haunt me on sleepless nights. Like ghosts, they hover over the bed and flit through my mind, making rest impossible.

But I've come to a decision, Lord. I'm not going to dwell on any of those things. Instead of counting sheep, I'm going to count my blessings. I'm going to try remembering each and every blessing from Your hand as far back as I can remember. So even if I am awake the rest of the night, we'll have a good time.

Amen.

Tired nature's sweet restorer, balmy sleep!

Edward Young

When I need strength . . .

Have you not heard?
The everlasting God, the LORD,
The Creator of the ends of the earth,
Neither faints nor is weary. . . .
He gives power to the weak,
And to those who have no might He increases strength.
Even the youths shall faint and be weary,
And the young men shall utterly fall,
But those who wait on the LORD
Shall renew their strength;
They shall mount up with wings like eagles,
They shall run and not be weary,
They shall walk and not faint.

ISAIAH 40:28-31 NKJV

I will boast . . . about my weaknesses, so that Christ's power
may rest on me. . . . For when I am weak, then I am strong.

2 CORINTHIANS 12:9-10

Come to me, all you who are weary and burdened, and I
will give you rest. Take my yoke upon you and learn from me,
for I am gentle and humble in heart, and you will find rest
for your souls. For my yoke is easy and my burden is light.

MATTHEW 11:28-30

. . . I will pray.

Heavenly Father,

There must be a mistake somewhere because I'm carrying a load too heavy for me. You know me, Father. I'm not that strong, and I don't seem to be getting stronger. Just the opposite is happening. Sometimes I think I can't face another day if I have to carry everything myself. Maybe I'm losing my courage too.

But when another day dawns, I know I can't quit. The people I love depend upon me to be strong. I'm carrying some burdens for them, too, and I can't lay them down.

Today, I'm putting all of my burdens in a basket of trust—trust in You and Your goodness. Please, Father, would You grab hold of the other handle? Will You help me haul these burdens and responsibilities up the hill? Just as I know I can't let others down, I know You won't let me down. Though I am weak, You are strong. Though I falter, Your step is steady and sure.

Thank You, Lord, for being the Strength of my life and my Burden-Lifter.

Amen.

When a man has no strength, if he leans on God,
he becomes powerful.

Dwight Lyman Moody

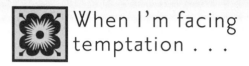

When I'm facing temptation . . .

[Jesus prayed] Do not lead us into temptation,
but deliver us from evil.
MATTHEW 6:13 NASB

[Jesus said] Keep watching and praying that you
may not enter into temptation; the spirit is willing,
but the flesh is weak.
MATTHEW 26:41 NASB

Control yourselves and be careful! The devil, your enemy,
goes around like a roaring lion looking for someone to eat.
Refuse to give in to him, by standing strong in your faith.
You know that your Christian family all over the world is
having the same kinds of suffering.
1 PETER 5:8-9 NCV

No temptation has overtaken you except such as is common to
man; but God is faithful, who will not allow you to be
tempted beyond what you are able, but with the
temptation will also make the way of escape,
that you may be able to bear it.
1 CORINTHIANS 10:13 NKJV

. . . I will pray.

Dear God,

I'm fighting the need to feel someone close to me. Desire creeps up behind me and whispers in my ear, making promises and singing a sweet song of lies. Funny thing: they are not all lies. There is just enough truth to keep me rationalizing. The temporary satisfaction never compensates for the pain—never. In the cold light of day when the pleasure has ended, I know I'll be sorry.

Of course, when I ask, You'll forgive me. Your forgiveness is precious, but I know You're disappointed in me. You hate to see me tasting poison time after time.

So this time I'm asking for help before I give in. Lead me away from temptation. Unmask its charms so I can see its true nature before I surrender. Let me see its price before the bill arrives.

Most of all, give me the strength to push it away. All-Powerful God, grant me Your strength to resist temptation.

Amen.

The whole effort—the object of—temptation is
to induce us to substitute something else for God.
To obscure God.

R. H. Stewart

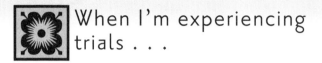

When I'm experiencing trials . . .

Count it all joy when you fall into various trials,
knowing that the testing of your faith produces patience.
But let patience have its perfect work, that you may be perfect
and complete, lacking nothing.

JAMES 1:2-4 NKJV

❀

Beloved, do not think it strange concerning the fiery trial
which is to try you, as though some strange thing happened to
you; but rejoice to the extent that you partake of Christ's
sufferings, that when His glory is revealed, you may also be
glad with exceeding joy.

1 PETER 4:12-13 NKJV

❀

[The Lord] reached down from heaven and took me and
drew me out of my great trials. He rescued me from deep
waters.

PSALM 18:16 TLB

❀

Anyone who meets a testing challenge head-on and manages
to stick it out is mighty fortunate. For such persons loyally in
love with God, the reward is life and more life.

JAMES 1:12 MSG

. . . I will pray.

Heavenly Father,

Why is it that all of life's troubles seem to come crashing down at the same time? Just when I think I can't handle anything else, here comes the next piece of faulty scaffolding, right on the head.

I shouldn't be surprised. This is the nature of life. But right now, I can't muster the strength I need to lift my head. I'm not sleeping well—some nights not at all. My mind races as I consider my life and how I can face these circumstances. This time, with so much of my life unraveling, I feel like I don't have any reserves. I can look only to You.

I am at the end of myself, Lord. I don't know how I can handle the trials in my life. So I ask You, God of mercy, to give me strength—physical, emotional, and spiritual. I know You walk through all of life with me—the good times and the not-so-good times—but please give me a sense of Your presence as I face these circumstances. Help me to become a stronger, more compassionate person as a result of my present suffering. And thank You for Your sustaining power and presence in my life.

Amen.

In this life we will encounter hurts and trials that we will not be able to change; we are just going to have to allow them to change us.

Ron Lee Davis

When I need wisdom . . .

We have not stopped praying for you and asking God to fill
you with the knowledge of his will through all spiritual
wisdom and understanding.

COLOSSIANS 1:9

If any of you is lacking in wisdom, ask God, who gives to all
generously and ungrudgingly, and it will be given you.

JAMES 1:5 NRSV

Happy is the person who finds wisdom,
the one who gets understanding.
Wisdom is worth more than silver;
it brings more profit than gold.
Wisdom is more precious than rubies;
nothing you could want is equal to it.
With her right hand wisdom offers you a long life,
and with her left hand she gives you riches and honor.

PROVERBS 3:13-16 NCV

The LORD says, "I will guide you along the best pathway for
your life. I will advise you and watch over you."

PSALM 32:8 NLT

. . . I will pray.

Dear Lord,

My mind feels muddled right now. I want to move forward, to do the right thing, but I don't have a sense of what that is. Is there an absolute "right thing"? I've talked with people about my options, but it's left me feeling even more confused. I know I'm the only one who can make this decision.

Isn't it ironic that I've asked others to pray for me as I've walked around consumed—weighing my options, running over at the mouth, losing sleep? From the very start, I could have been seeking wisdom from You. You see everything, know everything—past, present, and future. You also want what is best for me, and not necessarily what will make me happy. Maybe that's what has kept me from talking with You. Sometimes choosing the right thing isn't the easiest decision.

So I humbly ask You to help me. I ask for Your direction and for the clarity I need to know what that is. I pray that Your will can become my will, because I know that is the only way I can truly serve You and the people in my life.

Thank You for loving me, for wanting what's best. Thank You for Your wise guidance.

Amen.

Wisdom, awful wisdom! which inspects,
Discerns, compares, weighs, separates, infers,
Seizes the right, and holds it to the last.

Edward Young

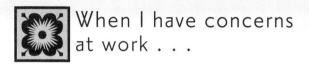 When I have concerns
at work . . .

*My life is worth nothing unless I use it for doing
the work assigned me by the Lord Jesus.*
ACTS 20:24 NLT

*In all the work you are doing, work the best you can. Work as
if you were doing it for the Lord, not for people. Remember
that you will receive your reward from the Lord, which he
promised to his people. You are serving the Lord Christ.*
COLOSSIANS 3:23-24 NCV

*Do your work with enthusiasm. Work as if you were serving
the Lord, not as if you were serving only men and women.*
EPHESIANS 6:7 NCV

*To enjoy your work and to accept your lot in life—
that is indeed a gift from God. The person who does that will
not need to look back with sorrow on his past,
for God gives him joy.*
ECCLESIASTES 5:19-20 TLB

. . . I will pray.

Heavenly Father,

I have that same feeling in the pit of my stomach that I used to have as a young girl on Sunday nights before school—but it's Tuesday night, and I'm a grown woman whose once-great job has now become an unsettling dilemma.

The anxiety is starting to get to me, and I don't know how to handle it. I'm not sleeping well, so I don't have the best coping skills—it's all I can do to get through the day. I know other people see how negative I've become. I don't want to poison the air around me. Do I start looking somewhere else, or should I stay? I've invested a lot of myself, and that makes this especially hard.

Lord, I ask You for the strength to overcome my negative attitude as I approach work and move through the business of my day. If I should stay, please give me the resolve I need to make the best of my situation. Help me to find meaning in my work and let go of the bitterness I've harbored. If it's time to move on, I ask for direction and peace. It's so good to know that You are with me no matter what the future holds for me here.

Amen.

A dairymaid can milk cows to the glory of God.

Martin Luther

God, be merciful to me;
On Thy grace I rest my plea;
In Thy vast, abounding grace,
My transgressions all erase.
Wash me wholly from my sin;
Cleanse from every ill within.

The Psalter

Prayers of Confession

Lifting My Voice to God
When I Need Forgiveness

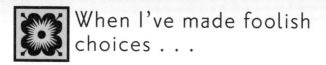 When I've made foolish
choices . . .

The LORD can control a king's mind as he controls a river;
he can direct it as he pleases.
PROVERBS 21:1 NCV

He shows how to distinguish right from wrong, how to find
the right decision every time. For wisdom and truth will enter
the very center of your being, filling your life with joy.
PROVERBS 2:9-10 TLB

You are right and you do right, GOD;
your decisions are right on target.
PSALM 119:137 MSG

Who are they that fear the LORD?
He will teach them the way that they should choose.
PSALM 25:12 NRSV

This day I call heaven and earth as witnesses against you
that I have set before you life and death, blessings and curses.
Now choose life, so that you and your children may live.
DEUTERONOMY 30:19

. . . I will pray.

Heavenly Father,

It would be convenient to blame someone else for the situation I'm in now. I've tried to rationalize the "whys" of reaching this point. But when I close my eyes at night, all I see is that neon flashing sign, "You did this to yourself," and then a final, condemning "again."

Since I have no idea how to undo the past, I have but two choices: to continue wallowing in my grief or to move forward with new intent. But how can I maintain that intention enough to keep me from making poor decisions? Honestly, I'm afraid to know what I must give up—what I need to change—in order to choose and act differently.

Lord, please reveal the truth to me about why I keep returning to the same patterns, making these choices that lead to nowhere good. I pray for the wisdom and willpower I need to do what is right even when it's not comfortable or convenient. I ask for forgiveness. I vow to weigh my life and pray more, not just when I've hit bottom, but as I'm living moment to moment, day to day.

I am grateful for the power of Your Spirit to renew my heart and mind.

Amen.

By the mercy of God we may repent a wrong
choice and alter the consequences by making
a new and right choice.

A. W. Tozer

When I've become critical and judgmental . . .

[Jesus said] Don't pick on people, jump on their failures, criticize their faults—unless, of course, you want the same treatment. That critical spirit has a way of boomeranging. It's easy to see a smudge on your neighbor's face and be oblivious to the ugly sneer on your own.

MATTHEW 7:1-3 MSG

The whole Law can be summed up in this one command: "Love others as you love yourself." But if instead of showing love among yourselves you are always critical and catty, watch out! Beware of ruining each other.

GALATIANS 5:14-15 TLB

Encourage one another and build up one another.

1 THESSALONIANS 5:11 NASB

Encourage one another day after day, as long as it is still called "Today," so that none of you will be hardened by the deceitfulness of sin.

HEBREWS 3:13 NASB

. . . I will pray.

Father God,

I've fallen into a common and destructive pattern of thinking. A counselor called it the "shadow syndrome." As I understand it, this is where a person continues to focus on someone else's faults until the negative grows to huge proportions and begins to overshadow everything positive. At that point, it's almost impossible to realistically see or know one's own heart.

Introspection hasn't been my strong suit, Lord—so I come before You knowing I need to examine myself. It doesn't take much for me to realize that I have harbored these unhappy, dark, and constantly critical thoughts. I admit that I haven't even tried to let them go. Instead, I've let them spread like poison through my heart and mind.

I ask, with a contrite heart, that You forgive me. Please also give me the courage to ask forgiveness from the one I've hurt. I pray for transformation—for my thoughts and my perspective. Help me to see the good in him—to approach him and others in my life with humility.

Thank You, Lord, for Your love and mercy.

Amen.

The faults of others are like headlights of an approaching car—they always seem more glaring than our own.

Author Unknown

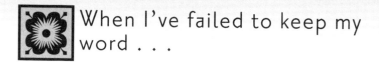

When I've failed to keep my word . . .

[The Lord commanded] If a man makes a promise to the
LORD or says he will do something special, he must keep his
promise. He must do what he said.

NUMBERS 30:2 NCV

❋

If you do not make the promise, you will not be guilty. You
must do whatever you say you will do, because you chose to
make the promise to the LORD your God.

DEUTERONOMY 23:22-23 NCV

❋

Keep your word even when it costs you.

PSALM 15:4 MSG

❋

O God, . . . help me never to tell a lie.

PROVERBS 30:7-8 TLB

❋

Love and truth form a good leader;
sound leadership is founded on loving integrity.

PROVERBS 20:28 MSG

. . . I will pray.

Heavenly Father,

I'm a walking disappointment—to myself and to the one I hurt by failing to keep my word. I feel sick about it. And worst of all, I look back now and realize it isn't the first time I've taken my promises too lightly, broken them too quickly, spoken too casually.

God, I know that You place high value on words. The way I trust Your promises, depend on You every time I have a need—I've taken that for granted, without thinking that You expected me to be as diligent to keep my own words. I've hurt a friend, but I've also sinned against You. I ask for Your forgiveness.

And where my friend is concerned, please help me know the right approach, the right words to say to restore this relationship. Help me to measure my words in the future, and give me strength to stand by them no matter what.

I do want to be more like You, Lord. I want to be true and certain and unwavering just as You, my heavenly Father, are true and certain and unwavering.

Thank You for being a God in whom I can trust.

Amen.

He who is slow in making a promise is most likely to be faithful in the performance of it.

Jean Jacques Rousseau

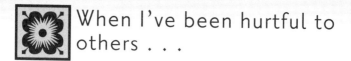
The tongue runs wild, a wanton killer. With our tongues we bless God our Father; with the same tongues we curse the very men and women he made in his image. Curses and blessings out of the same mouth! My friends, this can't go on. A spring doesn't gush fresh water one day and brackish the next, does it?

JAMES 3:8-11 MSG

[Jesus said] When you are offering your gift at the altar, if you remember that your brother or sister has something against you, leave your gift there before the altar and go; first be reconciled to your brother or sister, and then come and offer your gift.

MATTHEW 5:23-24 NRSV

Put these things out of your life: anger, bad temper, doing or saying things to hurt others, and using evil words when you talk. Do not lie to each other. You have left your old sinful life and the things you did before. You have begun to live the new life, in which you are being made new and are becoming like the One who made you.

COLOSSIANS 3:8-10 NCV

. . . I will pray.

Father God,

I pulled back the bow with full force and let it rip—poison arrows right into the heart. And the look on my friend's face let me know that I hit the mark. Now all I can think about is that look, and how ugly my heart must be to have said what I did. I didn't plan to be cruel, but I was so angry.

I know I need to apologize, but I don't know if anything can ever be the same. Once the words are out, there's no pulling them back. I was awful. My first urge is to make excuses for what I said, push old grievances to the surface. But that's simply wrong. Only humility on my part, divine intervention, and time can ease the blow of what I said.

So I ask You, God, to intervene and help us repair this breach I've caused. Please allow Your Word and Spirit to change me, and help me to be more controlled, to speak and act with kindness and wisdom.

I am grateful that, even when I am at my worst, You extend Your loving-kindness and mercy toward me.

Amen.

Cold words freeze people, and hot words scorch them, and bitter words make them bitter, and wrathful words make them wrathful. Kind words . . . soothe, and quiet, and comfort the hearer.

Blaise Pascal

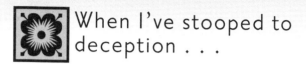

When I've stooped to deception . . .

Speaking the truth in love, we will in all things grow up into
him who is the Head, that is, Christ.
EPHESIANS 4:15

❀

Keep deception and lies far from me.
PROVERBS 30:8 NASB

❀

Listen to me! For I have important information for you.
Everything I say is right and true, for I hate lies and
every kind of deception.
PROVERBS 8:6-7 TLB

❀

He who speaks the truth gives honest evidence,
but a false witness utters deceit.
PROVERBS 12:17 RSV

❀

Putting away falsehood, let every one speak the truth with his
neighbor, for we are members one of another.
EPHESIANS 4:25 RSV

. . . I will pray.

Father in Heaven,

I have a sick feeling in the pit of my stomach that I can't shake. I should feel relieved. I've smoothed things over. Everyone thinks well of me. It must be my conscience—the part of me that gauges the means and not the end. I admit, the means were not exactly forthright—not altogether up-front.

It's plausible that I found myself in a position wherein I said some vague things or mislaid some facts. Really, what my inner gauge is telling me, Lord—what You know to be truth—is that I've lied. I've been deceptive in ways big and small. I did it to make myself look better. Now I'm sick over it. I have no peace.

Father, I know You hate deception, but You don't hate me. I can't say that for the people I've lied to, once they know I've been untruthful. Every fiber of my being is pulling me to continue the farce, but I know I must come clean. I need courage. I need strength. Thank You for forgiving me and seeing me through this mess of my own making.

Amen.

The essence of lying is in deception, not in words; a lie may be told by silence, by equivocation, by the accent on a syllable, by a glance of the eye attaching a peculiar significance to a sentence.

John Ruskin

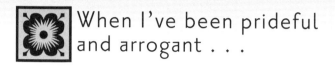

When I've been prideful and arrogant . . .

When pride comes, then comes disgrace;
but with the humble is wisdom.

PROVERBS 11:2 RSV

Pride goes before destruction and haughtiness before a fall.

PROVERBS 16:18 TLB

Lord, you know the hopes of humble people. Surely you will
hear their cries and comfort their hearts by helping them.

PSALM 10:17 TLB

Pride will ruin people,
but those who are humble will be honored.

PROVERBS 29:23 NCV

Pride leads to arguments; be humble,
take advice and become wise.

PROVERBS 13:10 TLB

. . . I will pray.

Heavenly Father,

She was just an acquaintance, someone I hardly knew, but I'll never forget her words. She said I act as if I'm superior—that I can't admit fault. She concluded by saying I don't respect people. I lashed back—said it was absolutely untrue. But something inside me is saying that I should take her words seriously—they have the ring of truth.

I know I'm not good at listening to what other people think. I don't accept criticism. I have tried to align myself with people of status at work and in my personal life. As I've reflected and prayed, I am reminded that my behavior is completely opposite of what Christ taught. I should value everyone—put others before myself. For the first time in a long time, I see myself as others must see me.

I pray to You, God, and ask forgiveness for the way I've acted—for what I've let myself become. I've put my reputation and personal interests above the interests of others. I ask You to help me see people as You see them. While I'm scared even to pray this, I ask You to reveal the intentions of my heart and strip it of pride and arrogance.

You are indeed a patient and merciful God.

Amen.

Pride is spiritual cancer; it eats the very possibility of love or contentment, or even common sense.

C. S. Lewis

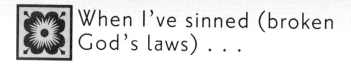# When I've sinned (broken God's laws) . . .

[Peter said] Everyone who believes in him receives
forgiveness of sins through his name.
ACTS 10:43 NRSV

Blessed are those whose iniquities are forgiven,
and whose sins are covered;
blessed is the one against whom the Lord
will not reckon sin.
ROMANS 4:7-8 NRSV

Keep your servant also from willful sins;
may they not rule over me.
Then will I be blameless,
innocent of great transgression.
PSALM 19:13

If we confess our sins, He is faithful and just to forgive us our
sins and to cleanse us from all unrighteousness.
1 JOHN 1:9 NKJV

. . . I will pray.

Dear Lord,

I have willfully and repeatedly done wrong. I deliberately broke a sacred commandment, broke a vow, and I need to stop. I haven't suffered any outward repercussions yet, though I sense the storm clouds building. I see how my sin is changing me—making me colder, less available, edgy. I know others sense this in me.

I'm at odds with my conscience—my spirit. I've taken a great step away from what I know is right. I'm scared, but I'm desperate to stop this sin. I'm afraid of failure, afraid of censure, terrified of being caught. Yet You already see—I can't go on pretending that You don't.

Holy God, I have broken trust and sinned against You. You have commanded us to follow Your Law, to keep our vows, to keep ourselves from sin. I confess my sin to You now with no reserve, knowing that mere confession isn't enough. I must repent, intend with all my heart to turn completely away from this sin. I will not dwell on what I've done, and I will not entertain even the mere thought of doing it again. That has been dangerous territory for me. Help me to follow Your Law.

You are a great and abundantly merciful God.

Amen.

Christ's death on the cross included a sacrifice for all our sins, past, present, and future. Every sin that you will ever commit has already been paid for.

Erwin W. Lutzer

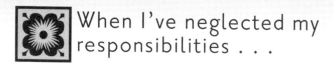

When I've neglected my responsibilities . . .

Don't try to avoid responsibility by saying you didn't know about it. For God knows all hearts, and he sees you.
PROVERBS 24:12 NLT

❋

Each person should judge his own actions and not compare himself with others. Then he can be proud for what he himself has done. Each person must be responsible for himself.
GALATIANS 6:4-5 NCV

❋

If God has given you leadership ability, take the responsibility seriously.
ROMANS 12:8 NLT

❋

Be very careful, then, how you live—not as unwise but as wise, making the most of every opportunity, because the days are evil.
EPHESIANS 5:15-16

❋

Discipline yourself for the purpose of godliness; for bodily discipline is only of little profit, but godliness is profitable for all things, since it holds promise for the present life and also for the life to come.
1 TIMOTHY 4:7-8 NAS

. . . I will pray.

Heavenly Father,

It's finally hit me! A successful life doesn't consist of random, frantic eleventh-hour sprints. What constitutes a responsible life is deliberate, consistent engagement (with some sprints). And that last definition does not apply to the way I live my life. I don't know if it ever has. That's largely why I haven't been able to keep up—why I've let personal, financial, and professional tasks slide.

I'd like to say, "Well, that's the way I am. I just function better at the last minute." But I'm a grown-up in a world with largely adult expectations. That's why certain grown-ups are not all that enthusiastic about me right now. I can't blame them. I need some serious help—starting with respect for myself and for others who count on me.

Lord, I ask You to first forgive my lack of discipline. I've put my momentary whims before my responsibilities. I ask You to help me to better focus and find balance in my life. I commit to live more deliberately, to engage in the moments of my day. With Your help, I know this is possible.

Thanks for being a God who cares about the details of my life.

Amen.

Character—the willingness to accept responsibility
for one's own life—is the source from which
self-respect springs.

Joan Didion

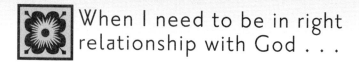# When I need to be in right relationship with God . . .

Cultivate your own relationship with God.
ROMANS 14:22 MSG

✻

Your fellowship with God enables you to gain a victory over the Evil One.
1 JOHN 2:14 MSG

✻

Draw near to God and He will draw near to you.
JAMES 4:8 NASB

✻

[Jesus said] Look! I have been standing at the door and I am constantly knocking. If anyone hears me calling him and opens the door, I will come in and fellowship with him and he with me.
REVELATION 3:20 TLB

✻

We can rejoice in our wonderful new relationship with God—all because of what our Lord Jesus Christ has done for us in making us friends of God.
ROMANS 5:11 NLT

. . . I will pray.

Dear Lord,

It's not that I've done anything overtly terrible. Nothing much has changed in the way I act or live, and yet I know something is wrong. It hits me when I stop—when my head hits the pillow at night.

Things aren't right between us, Lord. I've changed. I haven't prayed, aside from my obligatory dinner prayer. Even that has gone by the wayside lately. Really, I've been living my life as if You didn't exist. It's a fatal omission that's happened quite gradually as I've become busier—more preoccupied with the details of my life. I know You, and only You, give hope and meaning to my life. So why am I living as if this isn't true?

Though I haven't said it for a while, Lord, I love You. I'm glad to be Your child. You are the source of life and the only means by which I have purpose for living. You are great and holy, worthy of my respect, and certainly of acknowledgment as I go through my days. Forgive me, Lord, for drifting far from You. I want to make a new start with You.

Thank You for being a Father who welcomes the wanderer home.

Amen.

Christianity is not a religion, it is a relationship.
Robert B. Thieme

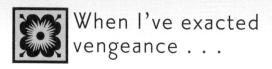# When I've exacted vengeance . . .

Don't say, "I'll pay you back for the wrong you did."
Wait for the LORD, and he will make things right.
PROVERBS 20:22 NCV

Beloved, never avenge yourselves, but leave room for the
wrath of God; for it is written, "Vengeance is mine, I will
repay, says the Lord." No, "if your enemies are hungry, feed
them; if they are thirsty, give them something to drink; for by
doing this you will heap burning coals on their heads." Do not
be overcome by evil, but overcome evil with good.
ROMANS 12:19-21 NRSV

Do not seek revenge or bear a grudge against one of your
people, but love your neighbor as yourself. I am the LORD.
LEVITICUS 19:18

[Love] is not touchy or fretful or resentful; it takes no account
of the evil done to it [it pays no attention to a suffered
wrong].
1 CORINTHIANS 13:5 AMP

. . . I will pray.

Heavenly Father,

I closely guarded my anger, harboring it through time, allowing it to grow. It became the force that drove my days and my energy to continue the plan to get him—to hurt him even more than he hurt me. Then I opened the gates and gave him the full force of my anger, making certain he wasn't the only one who knew the score.

Now I'm still alone and left with a burning anger. I believed that meting out my wrath would release it—leave me feeling light and free. Now, all it's fueling is bitterness. In a strange way, I don't want to let go of the bitterness because it's like admitting defeat. Yet I know it's stealing my happiness. I know I need to find a way to forgive; I should have started that process right from the start.

Lord, I know I didn't handle this situation well. I never talked to You about it; I just took matters into my own hands. Please forgive me, and help me to forgive as well. With Your help, I'd like to reach out to him before this cycle of hurt becomes our constant. Thank You, Lord, for a second chance.

Amen.

The noblest vengeance is to forgive.

Henry George Bohn

Make me an intercessor,
One who can really pray,
One of "the Lord's remembrancers"
By night as well as day.

Frances Ridley Havergal

Prayers of
Intercession

Lifting My Voice to God
on Behalf of Others

When my friend or family member is dealing with addiction . . .

He has delivered us from such a deadly peril, and he will deliver us. On him we have set our hope that he will continue to deliver us, as you help us by your prayers.

2 CORINTHIANS 1:10-11

❀

The praises of our fathers surrounded your throne; they trusted you and you delivered them. You heard their cries for help and saved them; they were never disappointed when they sought your aid.

PSALM 22:3-5 TLB

❀

Stretch out Your hand from above; Rescue me and deliver me out of great waters.

PSALM 144:7 NKJV

❀

[Jesus said] If the Son sets you free, you are free through and through.

JOHN 8:36 MSG

. . . I will pray.

Father God,

My heart is broken. I should have seen the signs—we all should have—but I suppose I didn't really want to know. Now I do, and they all point south. Addiction has taken someone I love with all my heart and transformed her into a stranger.

I've come to realize that I am powerless to do anything. That is excruciating. I've said and done what I could, but now I must step back and allow professionals to try. There are no guarantees. My best recourse is to pray. So You will be hearing from me a lot, Lord—most every waking moment. I know that her life and the lives of all of us who love her are in Your hands.

I also know that Your redemptive, healing, miracle-working hands are the best place for her. You love her even more than I do. Therefore, I ask You, Lord, for her deliverance from this terrible addiction—that You will break its power over her life and set her free.

Give her supernatural strength. Give wisdom to those who are working to help her. Help her to see You.

You are a God of sweet deliverance. And I give You thanks from the bottom of my heart.

Amen.

All the resources of the Godhead are at our disposal!

Jonathan Goforth

When my friend or family member is dealing with conflict . . .

Christ, who suffered for you, is your example.
Follow in his steps. He never sinned, and he never deceived
anyone. He did not retaliate when he was insulted.
When he suffered, he did not threaten to get even.
He left his case in the hands of God, who always judges fairly.

1 PETER 2:21-23 NLT

Don't repay evil for evil. Don't retaliate when people say
unkind things about you. Instead, pay them back with a
blessing. That is what God wants you to do,
and he will bless you for it. For the Scriptures say,
"If you want a happy life and good days,
keep your tongue from speaking evil,
and keep your lips from telling lies.
Turn away from evil and do good.
Work hard at living in peace with others.
The eyes of the Lord watch over those who do right,
and his ears are open to their prayers."

1 PETER 3:9-12 NLT

. . . I will pray.

Heavenly Father,

My friend is experiencing a lot of conflict in his life. I've been a sounding board, but that's as much as I feel comfortable offering him in this situation. It's not mine to repair. What I can do is pray for him right now, asking that You intervene in the situation to calm ruffled feathers, reignite love and respect, and restore the relationship.

I've watched as this conflict has robbed my friend of his joy, his rest, and his peace of mind. It has clouded—and continues to cloud—his judgment and perspective. Each day that this drags on will mean losses for him. So I kneel before the Author of peace and ask for a resolution.

Lord, thank You for what this friendship has meant in my life. Please give my friend the wisdom and grace he needs to deal with the situation, and guide him as he works to resolve it. I pray for the others involved as well. Work in all their lives to bring an even deeper harmony than they have ever known.

Amen.

Reconciliation is not weakness or cowardice.
It demands courage, nobility, generosity, sometimes
heroism, an overcoming of oneself rather than
of one's adversary.

Pope Paul VI

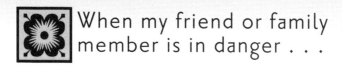# When my friend or family member is in danger . . .

GOD's my island hideaway,
keeps danger far from the shore.
PSALM 32:7 MSG

My life is well and whole, secure
in the middle of danger
Even while thousands
are lined up against me.
PSALM 55:18 MSG

My life is well and whole, secure
in the middle of danger
Even while thousands
are lined up against me.

Good Sense will scout ahead for danger,
Insight will keep an eye out for you.
PROVERBS 2:11 MSG

He is my strength, my shield from every danger.
I trusted in him, and he helped me.
PSALM 28:7 TLB

. . . I will pray.

Father God,

I realize we are all subject to the possibility of harm every time we get into our cars, travel by plane, or even eat at a restaurant. In truth, we never know what's around the corner, but we can't live paralyzed by fear. Lately, I have felt nearly undone with fear. Someone I love is in a situation that includes the possibility of life-threatening danger, and because he is so far away, I feel helpless to do anything about it.

I know You can see my loved one—no one is ever out of Your reach or too far away for You to see. You know where he is and what he's doing every moment of the day and night. You know where the dangers lie and where the safe havens are located. You know everything, Lord.

I now try to relinquish my fear as I entrust him to You. Please watch over him and those who are with him. Extend Your supernatural protection to cover him. I ask that You give him peace and a strong sense of Your presence.

Thank You for Your watchful care.

Amen.

The wise man in the storm prays to God,
not for safety from danger,
But for deliverance from fear.

Ralph Waldo Emerson

When my friend or family member goes through divorce . . .

The LORD is near to the brokenhearted
And saves those who are crushed in spirit.
PSALM 34:18 NASB

❀

The sacrifices of God are a broken spirit;
A broken and a contrite heart, O God, You will not despise.
PSALM 51:17 NASB

❀

Lord, you know the hopes of humble people. Surely you will
hear their cries and comfort their hearts by helping them.
PSALM 10:17 TLB

❀

Let your lovingkindness comfort me, just as you promised.
Surround me with your tender mercies, that I may live. For
your law is my delight.
PSALM 119:75-77 TLB

❀

Then they cried to the Lord in their troubles, and he helped
them and delivered them. He spoke, and they were healed.
PSALM 107:19-20 TLB

. . . I will pray.

Heavenly Father,

I wish desperately that they would give it another chance—engage in making their marriage work. But I've exhausted my words and emotions. It's painful and tiring walking through the motions of divorce with someone. You don't bear the full burden, but you experience the sorrow and frustration under a cold shadow, which leaves you feeling strangely alone.

I know these much-loved people will need support after the last papers have been signed. Make me sensitive to the grief that almost always accompanies divorce. I pray also for healing that allows this couple to put the past behind them and move on with their lives.

Heavenly Father, You are just and compassionate. You understand our weaknesses and forgive when we repent. Please work in the hearts of each of these precious people and help them rebuild their lives in ways that will honor You. Give them wisdom in dealing with their children. Help them as they grieve, and give them the grace to forgive one another.

Thank You for bringing good out of the hardest circumstances of life. You are a great God.

Amen.

When outward strength is broken, faith rests on the promises. In the midst of sorrow, faith draws the sting out of every trouble and takes out the bitterness from every affliction.

Robert Cecil

When my friend or family member is struggling with finances . . .

Many are the afflictions of the righteous,
But the LORD delivers him out of them all.
PSALM 34:19 NKJV

I know what it is to have little, and I know what it is to have
plenty. In any and all circumstances I have learned the secret
of being well-fed and of going hungry, of having plenty and of
being in need. I can do all things through him who
strengthens me.
PHILIPPIANS 4:12-13 NRSV

I have been young and now I am old,
Yet I have not seen the righteous forsaken
Or his descendants begging bread.
PSALM 37:25 NASB

A friend loves at all times,
and a brother is born for adversity.
PROVERBS 17:17

. . . I will pray.

Dear Lord,

I can see it on their faces—in their eyes and the tight, controlled way they hold their chins—stress is consuming them. I'm not really surprised. Struggling to make ends meet can rob you of sleep and the simple enjoyment of everyday life. I want so much to help, but money problems are private and personal. I know I'll need to tread lightly.

Show me what I can do, Lord. I'd be glad to help with the children or errands, or an anonymous gift. I'll be careful to listen for Your voice.

Lord, You are the great Provider and Comforter. I first ask that You would provide for my friends' basic needs. Please guide them as they make decisions about employment, lifestyle, and how best to apply the funds they have. Show them how to break any patterns that would continue to harm them.

I ask also that You would provide relief from their anxiety, knowing that You will supply everything they need. Help them to become better, wiser, even more generous people through this experience.

Thank You for Your provision every day.

Amen.

There is no situation so chaotic that God cannot
from that situation create something that is
surpassingly good. He did it at the creation. He did it
at the cross. He is doing it today.

Bishop Handley Carr Glyn Moule

When my friend or family member is experiencing grief . . .

The Spirit of the Sovereign LORD is upon me, because the LORD has appointed me to bring good news to the poor. He has sent me to comfort the brokenhearted. . . . He has sent me to tell those who mourn that the time of the LORD'S favor has come. . . . To all who mourn in Israel, he will give beauty for ashes, joy instead of mourning, praise instead of despair.

ISAIAH 61:1-3 NLT

Blessed be the God and Father of our Lord Jesus Christ, the Father of mercies and the God of all consolation, who consoles us in all our affliction, so that we may be able to console those who are in any affliction with the consolation with which we ourselves are consoled by God.

2 CORINTHIANS 1:3-4 NRSV

You have seen me tossing and turning through the night. You have collected all my tears and preserved them in your bottle! You have recorded every one in your book.

PSALM 56:8 TLB

Weep with those who weep.

ROMANS 12:15 RSV

. . . I will pray.

Heavenly Father,

My friend tells me it's like being punched in the stomach every morning. He wakes up, hopes it was a dream, and realizes too quickly that it wasn't. The person he loved is gone—does not exist any longer on this planet in any tangible form. I'm not sure what to say. No words seem adequate—and indeed aren't enough—to touch this pain.

I've come to see that grief is something that cannot be eased by other people. Even when we send cards, give food, and lend support—all beautiful gestures of caring—this is a road that each person must walk alone. And grief becomes an unpredictable specter, showing up when one least expects it, but nearly always in the quiet dark of night.

Lord, please extend Your loving comfort to my friend who is living with the immense weight of grief. Help him as he works to find a new normal in his life. I know that Your grace and loving-kindness can reach through this veil of sorrow. I pray especially for rest—for the good, peaceful sleep that has been elusive in these past days. Restore joy to him in due time, and please guide me as I try to support him.

Amen.

How shall we comfort those who weep?
By weeping with them.

Father Yelchaninov

When my friend or family member needs guidance . . .

In your unfailing love you will lead
the people you have redeemed.
In your strength you will guide them
to your holy dwelling.

EXODUS 15:13

He guides the humble in what is right
and teaches them his way.

PSALM 25:9

He guides the humble in what is right
and teaches them his way.

This God is our God for ever and ever;
he will be our guide even to the end.

PSALM 48:14

The LORD of hosts . . .
is wonderful in counsel and excellent in guidance.

ISAIAH 28:29 NKJV

. . . I will pray.

Father God,

I'm sure You hear this question every day: "Am I doing the right thing?" I ask it quite a bit myself. How do we know that we're living where we're supposed to live, working at the jobs we're supposed to have, doing the things in our personal lives that we're supposed to do? And how do we approach and gauge the choices we must make?

Conventional wisdom says that the best way to make wise decisions is to consult wise people, weigh them by our internal scales, look into God's Word—and pray, pray, pray every step of the way. So I am coming to You now, Lord, to do just that on behalf of a person in my life who desperately needs Your guidance.

God of wisdom, please help my friend. He's got such a big decision to make, and he's pretty worried about making the right one. I ask for Your guidance. I ask for peace once a path has been chosen. Whether it's through people, Your Word, or Your Spirit, please make the way clear.

I thank You for guiding Your children, giving them wisdom when they ask for it.

Amen.

God has led. God will lead. God is leading!

Richard C. Halverson

When my friend or family member needs emotional healing . . .

Floods of sorrow pour upon me like a thundering cataract. Yet day by day the Lord also pours out his steadfast love upon me, and through the night I sing his songs and pray to God who gives me life.

PSALM 42:7-8 TLB

He heals the brokenhearted And binds up their wounds.

PSALM 147:3 NKJV

My health fails; my spirits droop, yet God remains! He is the strength of my heart; he is mine forever!

PSALM 73:26 TLB

I will never lay aside your laws, for you have used them to restore my joy and health.

PSALM 119:93 TLB

Some people like to make cutting remarks, but the words of the wise soothe and heal.

PROVERBS 12:18 TLB

. . . I will pray.

Father God,

It is amazing how deeply past events can wound a person's spirit. I've known people who have carried the hurt from a broken relationship or mistreatment well into the later years of their lives. One little nudge and it erupts like a geyser—or it can seep like toxic water, contaminating the best of life.

Today, I bring before You my friend who is living with deep emotional pain. She can't seem to resolve it herself, though I know she's tried. I've attempted to help—to point to objective factors about her thinking and her situation—hoping something would "click." Others have too. But this hurt continues to poison her thinking, her view of herself, and her life.

God, thank You for my friend. You know more than I the extent of her pain and the true reasons for it. I ask You now—and I will continue to ask—for healing of her heart and spirit. I pray that You would direct her to the right person who can help her work through this situation so that she can emerge on the other side with a fresh perspective and joy.

Thank You for being a caring and compassionate God who heals the brokenhearted.

Amen.

Apt words have power to assuage
The tumors of a troubled mind
And are as balm to fester'd wounds.

John Milton

When my friend or family member needs physical healing . . .

Keep these thoughts ever in mind; let them penetrate deep within your heart, for they will mean real life for you, and radiant health.

PROVERBS 4:21-22 TLB

❀

He himself bore our sins in his body on the tree, that we might die to sin and live to righteousness. By his wounds you have been healed.

1 PETER 2:24 RSV

❀

[The Lord says] For you who honor me, goodness will shine on you like the sun, with healing in its rays.

MALACHI 4:2 NCV

❀

No doubt you know that God anointed Jesus of Nazareth with the Holy Spirit and with power. Then Jesus went around doing good and healing all who were oppressed by the Devil, for God was with him.

ACTS 10:38 NLT

. . . I will pray.

Heavenly Father,

It's horrible to watch someone you love suffer physically, especially when complications arise that compound pain and prolong healing, or when a condition is chronic. It's difficult for me not to ask the typical questions: Why this? Why him? Why now?

Yet, I know every one of us is susceptible to physical suffering at any turn. It's part of the human condition. So instead of becoming mired in questions or wrapped up in fear, I will talk to You, God, the Great Physician.

Father, someone I love is suffering and needs Your care. So I ask first for complete healing of this condition—that is my greatest desire. I acknowledge that You have complete power to do so at Your will.

I ask also for wisdom and insight for those who are caring for this dear one. I pray that You will give them the strength and energy not only to endure, but to overcome and become stronger as a result. I ask that You would provide for any needs that are not being met because of this illness.

Thank You for Your help and deliverance.

Amen.

Our Substitute bore both our sins and our sicknesses that we might be delivered from them.

F. F. Bosworth

When my friend or family member has a problem with infertility . . .

Delight yourself in the LORD
and he will give you the desires of your heart.
PSALM 37:4

❋

[Jesus said] Whatever you ask the Father in My name He
will give you. Until now you have asked nothing in My name.
Ask, and you will receive, that your joy may be full.
JOHN 16:23-24 NKJV

❋

He gives children to the childless wife, so that she becomes a
happy mother. Hallelujah!
PSALM 113:9 TLB

❋

Children are a gift from the LORD;
babies are a reward.
PSALM 127:3 NCV

❋

Where is the man who fears the Lord? . . .
He shall live within God's circle of blessing,
and his children shall inherit the earth.
PSALM 25:12-13 TLB

. . . I will pray.

Heavenly Father,

She is completely despondent. I didn't realize until recently how hard this is for them—trying to conceive and failing, month after month. I can see how this has engulfed her—left her depressed. At our age, we see babies everywhere we turn: a shower, a birthday, a christening. And what do mothers of babies talk about? Babies, of course.

I'm at a loss as to how to help her with this grief she's feeling about not having a baby. I don't want to be insensitive—do or say the wrong things—but I don't want to pretend this isn't happening either. The whole nature of this problem is complex because it's both extremely private and painfully public. After a while, it's hard to hide the baby that doesn't exist in your world.

God, You are the Author and Giver of life. You perform miracles beyond our comprehension. I ask that You work a great miracle in the lives of these people. Open the right doors for them, and gently guide them through this process of becoming parents. It is their deepest desire. But if You see fit not to change their circumstances, please extend Your comfort to them to soothe their grieving hearts.

Amen.

God views all of our requests in the context of His perfect will for our lives. Sooner or later, we understand that all prayers are answered prayers.

Andrea Garney

When my friend or family member is not in relationship with God . . . .

Since earliest times men have seen the earth and sky and all God made, and have known of his existence and great eternal power. So they will have no excuse [when they stand before God at Judgment Day].

ROMANS 1:20 TLB

[Jesus said] Plead with the Lord of the harvest to send out more laborers to help you, for the harvest is so plentiful and the workers so few.

LUKE 10:2 TLB

If they refuse to listen when you talk to them about the Lord, they will be won by your respectful, pure behavior. Your godly lives will speak to them better than any words.

1 PETER 3:1-2 TLB

[Jesus said] And I, as I am lifted up from the earth, will attract everyone to me and gather them around me.

JOHN 12:32 MSG

. . . I will pray.

Heavenly Father,

One of the most difficult things to come to terms with is the thought that people I like and love, who play an integral part in my life, have decided against You. Maybe they haven't done so overtly with a strident declaration, but more by omission—living as if You don't exist. Some, open to possibility, haven't landed in one camp or another.

The person who's on my mind right now is in the latter mode—not closed to the idea of a higher power (perhaps called God)—but not putting much effort into arriving at any conclusions. This is a stellar, "good" person who embodies so many of the so-called virtues of the Christian life—kindness, compassion, and selflessness. I know every person, however seemingly good, has a need for a real relationship with the one true God of the universe.

Loving and gracious Father, I pray for this person who doesn't yet know You. I ask You to ignite the spark that will lead her to seek Christ, and by truly seeking, come to have faith in Your power to redeem and give new life.

Amen.

Our task is to live our personal communion with Christ with such intensity as to make it contagious.

Paul Tournier

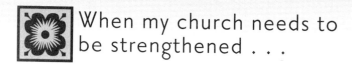# When my church needs to be strengthened . . .

The church . . . was strengthened; and encouraged by the Holy Spirit, it grew in numbers, living in the fear of the Lord.

ACTS 9:31

❀

When you come together, everyone has a hymn, or a word of instruction, a revelation, a tongue or an interpretation. All of these must be done for the strengthening of the church.

1 CORINTHIANS 14:26

❀

Conduct yourselves in a manner worthy of the gospel of Christ, so that . . . you are standing firm in one spirit, with one mind striving together for the faith of the gospel.

PHILIPPIANS 1:27 NASB

❀

Complete my joy by being of the same mind, having the same love, being in full accord and of one mind. Do nothing from selfishness or conceit, but in humility count others better than yourselves. Let each of you look not only to his own interests, but also to the interests of others.

PHILIPPIANS 2:2-4 RSV

. . . I will pray.

Heavenly Father,

Our church is in the midst of a shift, and people don't like it. You can easily sense the uncomfortable stir of people brushing up against change. Good people are talking, some leaving—and for what? A church that won't change?

Help me to remember that churches are flawed because people are flawed. It amounts to a work in progress, a living organism that won't reach maturity until Jesus Himself comes back for us. Until then, Your Holy Spirit is here each Sunday helping us through tough spots as we continue to worship You together.

God, I pray for the people who make up our congregation. I pray that You would expand their vision and increase their faith. I ask that You give the pastors and other staff the skill they need to lead our church through this time of transition, and the wisdom to know when to refrain from change for its own sake. Remind us often that the church's mission is that we should love and care for each other, help those who have need, and unite under one common purpose—to love and serve You.

Amen.

Church-goers are like coals in a fire.
When they cling together, they keep the flame aglow;
when they separate, they die out.

Billy Graham

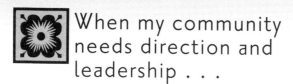 When my community needs direction and leadership . . .

When the righteous are in authority, the people rejoice.
PROVERBS 29:2 NKJV

❀

Unto us a child is born, unto us a son is given:
and the government shall be upon his shoulder.
ISAIAH 9:6 KJV

❀

Remind the believers to yield to the authority of rulers and
government leaders, to obey them, to be ready to do good.
TITUS 3:1 NCV

❀

I urge, then, first of all, that requests, prayers, intercession
and thanksgiving be made for everyone—for kings and all
those in authority, that we may live peaceful and quiet lives in
godliness and holiness.
1 TIMOTHY 2:1-2

❀

The king's heart is like channels of water in the hand of the
LORD; He turns it wherever He wishes.
PROVERBS 21:1 NASB

. . . I will pray.

Heavenly Father,

The reports I've heard on the national scene of crime and corruption have been unsettling, but I could at least view them from a distance. Recently, I've heard similar bleak and gruesome reports, but on our local news—rises in violent crime, and the jobless rate, underhanded city officials squandering taxpayers' money (or worse).

I want to take action, and I know there's plenty to do. Yet it's overwhelming to think about what it might take to enact real change. So, I'll start by coming to You, asking for Your guidance and committing myself to pray consistently for my community.

Work in the lives of individuals who live here, Lord. Give them faith and strength of character that they can pass on to their children. Protect our children from the things that rob them of their childhood. I pray that many people will come to know You and rely on You to guide their lives. Give us strong leaders with the courage to face and combat the problems in our community. Show me the work You have for me to do here.

I thank You for being a faithful, unchanging God. We place our trust in You.

Amen.

The government is us; we are the government,
you and I.

Theodore Roosevelt

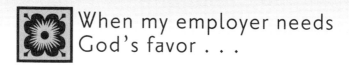

When my employer needs God's favor . . .

Whoever finds me [Wisdom] finds life,
And obtains favor from the LORD.
PROVERBS 8:35 NKJV

✿

[Abraham's servant said] O LORD, *the God of my master*
Abraham, please grant me success today,
and show lovingkindness to my master.
GENESIS 24:12 NASB

✿

Surely, O LORD, *you bless the righteous;*
you surround them with your favor as with a shield.
PSALM 5:12

✿

Send me a sign of your favor. When those who hate me see it
they will lose face because you help and comfort me.
PSALM 86:17 TLB

✿

Our power is based on your favor!
PSALM 89:17 TLB

. . . I will pray.

Heavenly Father,

Talk around the water cooler intimates that the company is looking shaky, which could mean layoffs, maybe just budget cuts. Everyone wonders, *Could it be me?* The bottom line: no one is truly safe.

You must be hearing that a lot from people in all types of professions and organizations. Almost everyone is feeling insecure about the future right now, particularly the status of their jobs within their companies. Loyalty on both sides, company to employee and vice versa, has been replaced with guerrilla survival tactics. It's hard to know whom to trust and how to pray for one's employer. Yet it's the right thing to do.

Lord, I thank You that I have my job. I ask You to guide those who are in positions to make decisions for our future. I pray that they may find faith in You if they don't already believe. I ask for Your blessing on the work that is done here. I pray that those making decisions can navigate through this patch skillfully, that jobs will be spared, and that we can remain successful and profitable.

You, Lord, reward diligence and honesty. May our efforts be worthy of Your favor.

Amen.

Almighty God, . . . we humbly beseech Thee that we may always prove ourselves a people mindful of Thy favor and glad to do Thy will.

George L. Locke

When I see injustice in the world around me . . .

Speak up for those who cannot speak for themselves,
for the rights of all who are destitute.
Speak up and judge fairly;
defend the rights of the poor and needy.
PROVERBS 31:8-9

He has told you, O man, what is good;
And what does the LORD require of you
But to do justice, to love kindness,
And to walk humbly with your God?
MICAH 6:8 NASB

He loves righteousness and justice;
the earth is full of the steadfast love of the LORD.
PSALM 33:4-5 RSV

The word of the LORD is upright;
and all his work is done in faithfulness.

Blessed (Happy, fortunate, to be envied) is he who
considers the weak and the poor; the Lord will deliver him
in the time of evil and trouble.
PSALM 41:1 AMP

. . . I will pray.

Heavenly Father,

We are privy to events as they unfold all over the globe through modern media. We get flashes of information, glimpse pictures that reveal the human condition at its best and worst. The latter often stems from oppression, poverty, elitism, and outright dictatorship. Lately I've seen more than snatches, and the injustice is appalling.

I find it tempting to default to asking, "God, where are You?" Yet I know that amidst the gravest cases of man's inhumanity to man, You are still present in the lives of individuals and perhaps working in ways we could never discern from a distance. I know Your heart is grieved over those who are helpless and oppressed—the least of these. And I look to You now for guidance to respond in a way that's pleasing to You.

Give me a compassionate heart, God, and direct me each day to ways I can help. Don't allow me to turn my back because the job is so great. Show me the part that I can manage with Your help. Thank You for allowing me to join You as You shine Your light of hope in the darkest corners of the earth.

Amen.

Man's capacity for justice makes democracy possible;
but man's inclination to injustice
makes democracy necessary.

Reinhold Niebuhr

When my nation needs direction and leadership . . .

*[The Lord said] If my people who are called by my name
humble themselves, and pray and seek my face, and turn from
their wicked ways, then I will hear from heaven,
and will forgive their sin and heal their land.*

2 Chronicles 7:14 rsv

Blessed is the nation whose God is the Lord.

Psalm 33:12 kjv

I help kings to govern and rulers to make fair laws.

Proverbs 8:15 ncv

*When a country is lawless, it has one ruler after another;
but when it is led by a man with understanding and
knowledge, it continues strong.*

Proverbs 28:2 ncv

*Loyalty and truth keep a king in power;
he continues to rule if he is loyal.*

Proverbs 20:28 ncv

. . . I will pray.

Father God,

I look around, and it's difficult to believe that I live in a Christian nation. Ungodliness abounds. The list of perversities and corruption, and evil, is far too long to enumerate here. Besides, You see it much more clearly than I—and it must break Your heart.

Lord, I lift my nation to You. I ask for mercy, for forgiveness, for direction, and for godly leadership. I ask that You would discern hearts and expose those whose agenda is greed and selfishness. I pray that You would raise up leaders fit to lead this nation in the way You intended.

Show me, too, Lord, how to do my part. Point out ways I can be a voice for godliness in this country. If that is to be here on my knees, help me to do that with fervor and constancy. If Your purposes are served by taking me outside my home to be a voice for You, open doors of opportunity and I will step through them. I'm ready to work, Lord, to put my actions behind my prayers. Thank You, Lord, for Your answers.

Amen.

Grant that I may not pray alone with the mouth;
help me that I may pray from the depths of my heart.

Martin Luther

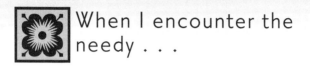

When I encounter the needy . . .

Blessed are those who help the poor.
PROVERBS 14:21 NLT

✿

*If you help the poor, you are lending to the LORD
—and he will repay you!*
PROVERBS 19:17 NLT

✿

Whoever gives to the poor will lack nothing.
PROVERBS 28:27 NRSV

✿

*If a brother or sister is naked and lacks daily food, and one of
you says to them, "Go in peace; keep warm and eat your fill,"
and yet you do not supply their bodily needs, what is the good
of that? So faith by itself, if it has no works, is dead.*
JAMES 2:15-17 NRSV

✿

*There will always be poor people in the land. Therefore I
command you to be openhanded toward your brothers and
toward the poor and needy in your land.*
DEUTERONOMY 15:11

. . . I will pray.

Heavenly Father,

I read about it all the time—so many people living in the most horrible conditions—without running water, reliable shelter, decent sanitation. They are forced to scrounge for food. And I'm not talking about those who have been temporarily displaced by natural disasters. These are people who live this way all the time. Their faces have an almost eerie, hollow look, as if they are only partially alive.

This breaks my heart, Lord, and if it breaks mine, it must break Yours even more. These people are precious to You. They are created in Your image, yet they lack even the barest necessities of life. I have no idea why this is so, or what I can possibly do to change the lot of even more of these suffering souls.

Lord, I ask You to speak to me. Show me what I can do, even if it is only a tiny drop in that huge ocean of humanity. Give me a name to pray for, a child to support, a heart that needs to feel the warmth of human love. Show me how to reach out in Your name to those in great need.

Amen.

What does love look like? It has hands to help others.
It has feet to hasten to the poor and needy. It has
eyes to see misery and want. It has ears to hear the
sighs and sorrows of men. That is what love looks like.

Saint Augustine of Hippo